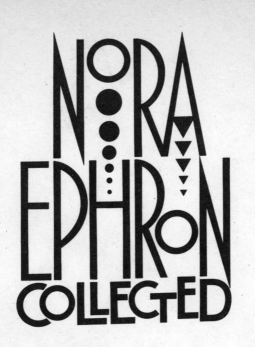

NORA
EPHRON
COLLECTED

NORA EPHRON

AVON BOOKS ◆ NEW YORK

NORA EPHRON COLLECTED is an original publication of Avon Books, and while portions of this work have previously appeared in other sources, this is the first time this collection has appeared in one volume.

Portions of this book have appeared in *Esquire* magazine, *New York* magazine, *The New York Times Magazine*, *The New York Times Book Review*, *The Dial*, and *Rolling Stone*.

Grateful acknowledgment is made to the Viking Press, Inc. for permission to reprint ten lines of poetry from *The Portable Dorothy Parker*. Copyright 1926, renewed 1954 by Dorothy Parker.

"The Mink Coat" was first published in the December 1975 issue of *Esquire* magazine.

"When Harry Met Sally dot dot dot" first appeared in the published screenplay of *When Harry Met Sally . . .*, as an introduction (Knopf, 1990).

AVON BOOKS
A division of
The Hearst Corporation
105 Madison Avenue
New York, New York 10016

First Avon Books Trade Printing: March 1991

AVON TRADEMARK REG. U.S. PAT. OFF. AND IN OTHER COUNTRIES, MARCA REGISTRADA, HECHO EN U.S.A.

Printed in the U.S.A.

OPM   10   9   8   7   6   5   4   3   2   1

C**O**NTENTS

CONTENTS

INTRODUCTION

FOR a while there, I wrote essays. First I wrote them about women, and they were collected in *Crazy Salad*. Then I wrote about the press, and they became *Scribble Scribble*. And then I wrote a few more.

Most of the essays in this collection were written when I was a columnist for *Esquire* magazine. Which is a monthly. I was very happy writing in a monthly. Years earlier, when I was a reporter at a daily newspaper, I was offered a twice-a-week column. The managing editor very nicely gave me several weeks to write a few. This was an absolutely impossible task for me for two reasons: first, I was too young to write a column; and second, I simply did not have two opinions a week. I am stunned at my friends who write columns in newspapers for many reasons—but mostly because I can't imagine how they have so many opinions. Well, actually, I don't have to imagine it—I know. Every thing that is set before them, every book, every newspaper article, every English muffin bristles with the possibility of inspiring 850 words, and I watch them as their eyes dart here and there, as they wonder, is there a column in this, am I missing a column in that, have I just said something I should write down, has someone at the table just said something I should write down. Their lives are a misery, if you ask me, but I salute them.

In any case, writing for a monthly required me to have only twelve opinions a year, which turned out to be about right. (In truth, it turned out to be about one too many, but you can always wing one opinion a year.) Also, monthly magazines have huge lead times; they require your copy three months before it's going to appear in print. This frees you from one of the worst problems any essayist has—which is of being wrong about something. You have time on almost any subject to let some other columnist be wrong. You have time to let the dust settle. You have distance—and distance almost always makes you a little smarter.

Writing a column imposes an interesting discipline—it forces you to put yourself up against a subject, forces you to have an opinion about it, forces you to make the opinion coherent and shapely. One of the reasons I wanted to write about women back there when I did was that I was afraid that if I didn't, I would drift through the ferment of the women's movement with the luxurious detachment of the reporter. I'm not suggesting that journalists don't have opinions, you understand; what I'm suggesting is that if you're simply reporting on something, you aren't forced to make your opinions as clearly known to yourself as you are when you're writing essays. For years, I believed that this detached stance was a natural one for me. My first collection of articles was called *Wallflower at the Orgy*, an expression that seemed perfectly to sum up what I felt as a journalist—I always seemed to be at a perfectly wonderful party where people were laughing and dancing and having sex, and I was on the sidelines taking notes on it. This was an extremely comfortable place for me to be, I must tell you that; but it became clear to me at a certain point that it wouldn't do. I was living through what seemed to me to be an important period for women, and it seemed entirely possible that unless I wrote about it in a way that forced me to decide what I thought about it, I would emerge from it with nothing more than a reporter's insights. A reporter's insights, in case you are interested, usually consist of a series of contradictory points (on the one hand, blah blah blah, but on the other hand, blah blah blah) climaxed by the following statement, which is meant to sound insightful but which is actually only an evasion: "I found it very (choose one: interesting/compelling/

fascinating) but I had problems with its (methodology/technique/approach)." This is the way most reporters respond to everything from wars to political movements to scoops by other reporters.

I see here that a bit of hostility toward journalism is starting to seep into this introduction. I hadn't meant to write about that; nonetheless, it's true that in recent years, my hopelessly-besotted infatuation with journalism has waned, almost to the point of extinction. The point, though, is that most of the pieces in this book were written by a journalist. Some of them I believe as sincerely as the day I finished writing them, and some of them were written by someone I used to be. In any case, here they are.

October, 1990

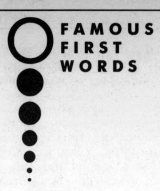

HERE is what interests me about Donald Trump: He wants
to be famous. He wants people to talk about him. He wants
people to notice him. He wants people to write about him.
He wants people to ask him for autographs and recognize
him and invade his privacy; not that he seems to have any
privacy; he doesn't even seem to have a single solitary
thought he manages to keep to himself, so perhaps there's
no privacy to invade. Perhaps that's the secret. Who knows?
It doesn't matter. I tip my hat to Donald Trump, because
except for an occasional churlish moment he seems to be
genuinely enjoying the experience of fame in a way that no
one in his right mind ever does, and the fact that he therefore
seems not to have any sense or intelligence or taste whatsoever is beside the point. *The man has adapted.*

Well, maybe he hasn't. Maybe he has spent his whole life
waiting for the light to shine on him. But look at him: look
how happy he is in his Trumphood; look how merrily he
floats in his Trumpdom; look how brightly he wallows in his
Trumpness. You just can't imagine him whining or complaining about any of it; you can't imagine him expecting to
be treated as if he were a normal person (if he ever was one).
That's the glory of Trump: you'll never find him behaving

like other famous people. You know the ones I mean, the fame victims who are constantly complaining about The Price You Pay. They're constantly trying to tell you this isn't what they meant at all; they're constantly behaving as if all this happened to them by accident; they're constantly insisting that they bleed like everyone else and their sinks leak like everyone else's and they have feelings like everyone else. They don't get it at all. *They're not like everyone else.* They're famous. They check into hotels and there are Belgian chocolates waiting on their beds. They go to movies and they don't have to stand on line. They get invited to wonderful parties, the kind you have waited your entire life to be invited to, and then they don't even go if they don't feel like it. Do they tell you about this? Do they mention the Concorde? Do they reveal that there is a special room for famous people at the Department of Motor Vehicles? No, indeed. They're too busy complaining among themselves about the downside, and pretending to the rest of the world that they are exactly the same people they always were.

There are five stages of fame: denial, anger, negotiation, acceptance, and death. These stages are virtually the same as the five stages of terminal illness.

Years ago, it was possible to achieve a level of celebrity somewhere beneath the level of outright fame. A pleasant level of celebrity if you will, the kind that guaranteed you a reservation or a ringside seat, a level of celebrity with no downside. This is the level of fame Giorgio Armani is apparently referring to in a new magazine called *Fame:* "Fame," he says, "is being in a foreign country, hailing a taxi, getting in, and the driver already knows your name." (If you believe Giorgio Armani still takes cabs, you'll believe anything; the reason the driver knows your name, Giorgio, is that he's a limousine driver, and your name is written on the voucher.) But these days, because of the huge public appetite for gossip and the vast amount of print space and broadcasting time devoted to the subject, the sort of person who might never have been heard of in the past and who is not even particularly interesting—a writer, television executive, agent, editor, real estate developer, or investment banker— can find himself suddenly famous. And he discovers, to his shock, that a bland, pleasant form of fame like the one Armani speaks of no longer exists: the moment a person ceases to be obscure he is catapulted straight into the big time, and after only a minute or two of the good stuff, and after only five or six minutes of denial, he's looking directly at the underbelly, right into the maw. Staring straight back at him are thousands of journalists who, having just made him famous, are now ready to follow up by trashing him and making his life a misery. They'll print anything whether it's true or not, nothing personal, that's how it is, they have space to fill, nobody asked you to become famous so don't blame them, what goes up must come down and the sooner the better.

These journalists are the primary reason why famous people get so angry. The famous person in the Second Stage of fame has lost control of his self-image, and it makes him so mad that he fails to acknowledge (1) that he wanted to be famous in the first place and (2) that there is anything good about being famous, like, for instance, being rich, which often accompanies it. The famous person in the Second Stage behaves as if he were as innocent as that poor guy in San Francisco who saved Gerald Ford's life and thus became the only genuine fame victim of our time. If you ask a famous person in the Second Stage, "If you never wanted to be famous, what were you doing on *The Tonight Show*?" he will answer that he did it only because his publicist told him he should, and then he will go on to talk about how inaccurate and irresponsible journalists are (which he is right about, but no one ever listens because he so clearly has an ax to grind); how mean people are (which he is also right about); and how he never wanted to be famous, he only wanted to be successful (which he is wrong about; the truth is, he wanted to be famous but he didn't want to pay the price for it).

A famous person in an acute phase of the Second Stage hits photographers.

The transition from the Second Stage to the Third Stage of fame—negotiation—is usually accomplished with the aid of a publicist. Publicists like to tell clients that there is something called good publicity, and that it can be had as a result of carefully orchestrated charitable episodes. The pioneer publicist in this area was a man named Ivy Lee, who convinced John D. Rockefeller that if he went around handing out dimes to little children, the press would ignore his reputation as an oil profiteer.

The famous person thus sets out to be good. His pathetic hope is that he will log something on the credit side of the ledger, something that will keep the bastards from looking through his garbage, something that will ensure that the next writer who is tempted to take a poke at him will be instead overwhelmed by admiration for his good works. Years ago, the most effective way for a celebrity to cloak himself in goodness was to buy a lesser disease, preferably one that primarily affected children; but after a while all the lesser diseases were taken, and famous people were forced to move on to other things: donating $10 million to the Metropolitan Museum, providing low-cost housing for the homeless (particularly trendy among unpopular real estate developers), boycotting South Africa, counseling AIDS patients, taking underprivileged children to baseball games, and, on the personal side, adopting an Asian orphan. Perhaps the most brilliant of the current forms of doing good is the rock concert for charity, which attests to the selflessness of the participant while simultaneously increasing his fame.

A movie star in the Third Stage of fame does not necessarily have to give money away to charity; he can choose an alternative form of self-abnegation—namely, working in the theater, preferably in a limited run of a play about the Vietnam War.

We should probably take special note here of Jack Nicholson, who is the epitome of the man who has learned to accept fame. Here is how Nicholson does it: He comes to town and photographers try to take his picture. He lets them take his picture. He keeps his dark glasses on and gives them that smile. When the photographers have shot more pictures of him than they can possibly sell, he stands there and lets them shoot more pictures. Several days pass in this manner. Hundreds more pictures are taken of Jack Nicholson going in and out of sporting events and restaurants and hotels. Finally the photographers have enough pictures of Jack Nicholson, and he gets his life back.

"I associate being recognized with being dead," says Harold Brodkey. You know who Harold Brodkey is—the man of letters, the famous author of the most famous unpublished novel of our time. Can this Harold Brodkey be the same Harold Brodkey who was recently featured, along with his wife, as a Couple in *People* magazine? Can this be Harold Brodkey, actually posing for a picture in *People* magazine while having his hair cut in his kitchen? Can this be Harold Brodkey, telling the writer from *People* that he and his wife are so dependent on one another that they have made a decision to be buried in a double coffin? Is this your idea of discretion, Harold? Is this your idea of hiding your light under a barrel? And what is a double coffin anyway, and how does it work? Do you have to be dug up later if you're the one who dies first? Do you have to die simultaneously? Is there a little hatch in the coffin, like the top of a Cuisinart, a pet door to eternity if you will, so that you can add what's left of the other person later on and mix them all up together in a big king-size bed in the ground? I don't know, but I long to find out, and I feel certain that I will, particularly if I keep reading Liz Smith's column, where Brodkey's remark on recognition and death appeared. Meanwhile, I salute Harold Brodkey for being the first man to attain the Fifth Stage of fame while still alive.

"Hey, life is life," says Donald Trump. *Famous people, are you listening?* "We're here for a short time," he says. The man is a goddamn philosopher. "When we're gone, most people don't care, and in some cases they're quite happy about it." Being famous means you can say things like that and actually get quoted in *Time* magazine. What more is there to say? So pull up your socks, famous people. Smile at the birdie. Your life is no longer your own. Big deal. Who do you think you are, anyway? What right do you have? The public has a right, not you. You asked for it, and here it is. Step right up. Fame is a calamity—that's a Turkish proverb and it's as old as the hills. So have a drink. Enjoy the party. The joke's on you, so you might as well have the last laugh.

June, 1989

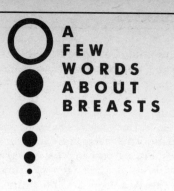

A FEW WORDS ABOUT BREASTS

HAVE to begin with a few words about androgyny. In grammar school, in the fifth and sixth grades, we were all tyrannized by a rigid set of rules that supposedly determined whether we were boys or girls. The episode in *Huckleberry Finn* where Huck is disguised as a girl and gives himself away by the way he threads a needle and catches a ball—that kind of thing. We learned that the way you sat, crossed your legs, held a cigarette, and looked at your nails—the way you did these things instinctively was absolute proof of your sex. Now obviously most children did not take this literally, but I did. I thought that just one slip, just one incorrect cross of my legs or flick of an imaginary cigarette ash would turn me from whatever I was into the other thing; that would be all it took, really. Even though I was outwardly a girl and had many of the trappings generally associated with girldom— a girl's name, for example, and dresses, my own telephone, an autograph book—I spent the early years of my adolescence absolutely certain that I might at any point gum it up. I did not feel at all like a girl. I was boyish. I was athletic, ambitious, outspoken, competitive, noisy, rambunctious. I had scabs on my knees and my socks slid into my loafers and I could throw a football. I wanted desperately not to be that way, not to be a mixture of both things, but instead just one, a girl, a definite indisputable girl. As soft and as pink as a nursery. And nothing would do that for me, I felt, but breasts.

I was about six months younger than everyone else in my class, and so for about six months after it began, for six months after my friends had begun to develop (that was the word we used, develop), I was not particularly worried. I would sit in the bathtub and look down at my breasts and know that any day now, any second now, they would start growing like everyone else's. They didn't. "I want to buy a bra," I said to my mother one night. "What for?" she said. My mother was really hateful about bras, and by the time my third sister had gotten to the point where she was ready to want one, my mother had worked the whole business into a comedy routine. "Why not use a Band-Aid instead?" she would say. It was a source of great pride to my mother that she had never even had to wear a brassiere until she had her fourth child, and then only because her gynecologist made her. It was incomprehensible to me that anyone could ever be proud of something like that. It was the 1950s, for God's sake. Jane Russell. Cashmere sweaters. Couldn't my mother see that? *I am too old to wear an undershirt.* Screaming. Weeping. Shouting. "Then don't wear an undershirt," said my mother. "But I want to buy a bra." "What for?"

I suppose that for most girls, breasts, brassieres, that entire thing, has more trauma, more to do with the coming of adolescence, with becoming a woman, than anything else. Certainly more than getting your period, although that, too, was traumatic, symbolic. But you could see breasts; they were there; they were visible. Whereas a girl could claim to have her period for months before she actually got it and nobody would ever know the difference. Which is exactly what I did. All you had to do was make a great fuss over having enough nickels for the Kotex machine and walk around clutching your stomach and moaning for three to five days a month about The Curse and you could convince anybody. There is a school of thought somewhere in the women's lib/women's mag/gynecology establishment that claims that menstrual cramps are purely psychological, and I lean toward it. Not that I didn't have them finally. Agonizing cramps, heating-pad cramps, go-down-to-the-school-nurse-and-lie-on-the-cot cramps. But, unlike any pain I had ever suffered, I adored the pain of cramps, welcomed it, wallowed in it, bragged about it. "I can't go. I have cramps." "I can't do that. I have cramps." And most of all, gigglingly, blushingly: "I can't swim. I have cramps." Nobody ever used the hard-core word. Menstruation. God, what an awful word. Never that. "I have cramps."

The morning I first got my period, I went into my mother's bedroom to tell her. And my mother, my utterly-hateful-about-bras mother, burst into tears. It was really a lovely moment, and I remember it so clearly not just because it was one of the two times I ever saw my mother cry on my account (the other was when I was caught being a six-year-old klep-tomaniac), but also because the incident did not mean to me what it meant to her. Her little girl, her firstborn, had finally become a woman. That was what she was crying about. My reaction to the event, however, was that I might well be a woman in some scientific, textbook sense (and could at least stop faking every month and stop wasting all those nickels). But in another sense—in a visible sense—I was as androgynous and as liable to tip over into boyhood as ever.

I started with a 28 AA bra. I don't think they made them any smaller in those days, although I gather that now you can buy bras for five-year-olds that don't have any cups what-soever in them; trainer bras they are called. My first brassiere came from Robinson's Department Store in Beverly Hills. I went there alone, shaking, positive they would look me over and smile and tell me to come back next year. An actual fitter took me into the dressing room and stood over me while I took off my blouse and tried the first one on. The little puffs stood out on my chest. "Lean over," said the fitter. (To this day, I am not sure what fitters in bra departments do except to tell you to lean over.) I leaned over, with the fleeting hope that my breasts would miraculously fall out of my body and into the puffs. Nothing.

"Don't worry about it," said my friend Libby some months later, when things had not improved. "You'll get them after you're married."

"What are you talking about?" I said.

"When you get married," Libby explained, "your husband will touch your breasts and rub them and kiss them and they'll grow."

That was the killer. Necking I could deal with. Intercourse

I could deal with. But it had never crossed my mind that a man was going to touch my breasts, that breasts had something to do with all that, petting, my God, they never mentioned petting in my little sex manual about the fertilization of the ovum. I became dizzy. For I knew instantly—as naïve as I had been only a moment before—that only part of what she was saying was true: the touching, rubbing, kissing part, not the growing part. And I knew that no one would ever want to marry me. I had no breasts. I would never have breasts.

My best friend in school was Diana Raskob. She lived a block from me in a house full of wonders. English muffins, for instance. The Raskobs were the first people in Beverly Hills to have English muffins for breakfast. They also had an apricot tree in the back, and a badminton court, and a subscription to *Seventeen* magazine, and hundreds of games, like Sorry and Parcheesi and Treasure Hunt and Anagrams. Diana and I spent three or four afternoons a week in their den reading and playing and eating. Diana's mother's kitchen was full of the most colossal assortment of junk food I have ever been exposed to. My house was full of apples and peaches and milk and homemade chocolate-chip cookies—which were nice, and good for you, but-not-right-before-dinner-or-you'll-spoil-your-appetite. Diana's house had nothing in it that was good for you, and what's more, you could stuff it in right up until dinner and nobody cared. Bar-B-Q potato chips (they were the first in them, too), giant bottles of ginger ale, fresh popcorn with melted butter, hot fudge sauce on Baskin-Robbins jamoca ice cream, powdered-sugar doughnuts from Van de Kamp's. Diana and I had been best friends since we were seven; we were about equally popular in school (which is to say, not particularly), we had about the same success with boys (extremely intermittent), and we looked much the same. Dark. Tall. Gangly.

It is September, just before school begins. I am eleven years old, about to enter the seventh grade, and Diana and I have not seen each other all summer. I have been to camp and she has been somewhere like Banff with her parents. We are meeting, as we often do, on the street midway between our two houses, and we will walk back to Diana's and eat junk and talk about what has happened to each of us that summer. I am walking down Walden Drive in my jeans and my father's shirt hanging out and my old red loafers with the socks falling into them and coming toward me is . . . I take a deep breath . . . a young woman. Diana. Her hair is curled and she has a waist and hips and a bust and she is wearing a straight skirt, an article of clothing I have been repeatedly told I will be unable to wear until I have the hips to hold it up. My jaw drops, and suddenly I am crying, crying hysterically, can't catch my breath sobbing. My best friend has betrayed me. She has gone ahead without me and done it. She has shaped up.

Here are some things I did to help:
Bought a Mark Eden Bust Developer.
Slept on my back for four years.
Splashed cold water on them every night because some French actress said in *Life* magazine that that was what *she* did for her perfect bustline.
Ultimately, I resigned myself to a bad toss and began to wear padded bras. I think about them now, think about all those years in high school I went around in them, my three padded bras, every single one of them with different-sized breasts. Each time I changed bras I changed sizes: one week nice perky but not too obtrusive breasts, the next medium-sized slightly pointy ones, the next week knockers, true knockers; all the time, whatever size I was, carrying around this rubberized appendage on my chest that occasionally crashed into a wall and was poked inward and had to be poked outward—I think about all that and wonder how anyone kept a straight face through it. My parents, who normally had no restraints about needling me—why did they say nothing as they watched my chest go up and down? My friends, who would periodically inspect my breasts for signs of growth and reassure me—why didn't they at least counsel consistency?

And the bathing suits. I die when I think about the bathing suits. That was the era when you could lay an uninhabited bathing suit on the beach and someone would make a pass at it. I would put one on, an absurd swimsuit with its enormous bust built into it, the bones from the suit stabbing me in the rib cage and leaving little red welts on my body, and there I would be, my chest plunging straight downward absolutely vertically from my collarbone to the top of my suit and then suddenly, wham, out came all that padding and material and wiring absolutely horizontally.

Buster Klepper was the first boy who ever touched them. He was my boyfriend my senior year of high school. There is a picture of him in my high-school yearbook that makes him look quite attractive in a Jewish, horn-rimmed-glasses sort of way, but the picture does not show the pimples, which were air-brushed out, or the dumbness. Well, that isn't really fair. He wasn't dumb. He just wasn't terribly bright. His mother refused to accept it, refused to accept the relentlessly average report cards, refused to deal with her son's inevitable destiny in some junior college or other. "He was tested," she would say to me, apropos of nothing, "and it came out a hundred and forty-five. That's near-genius." Had the word "underachiever" been coined, she probably would have lobbed that one at me, too. Anyway, Buster was really very sweet—which is, I know, damning with faint praise, but there it is. I was the editor of the front page of the high-school newspaper and he was editor of the back page; we had to work together, side by side, in the print shop, and that was how it started. On our first date, we went to see *April Love*, starring Pat Boone. Then we started going together. Buster had a green coupe, a 1950 Ford with an engine he had hand-chromed until it shone, dazzled, reflected the image of anyone who looked into it, anyone usually being Buster polishing it or the gas-station attendants he constantly asked to check the oil in order for them to be overwhelmed by the sparkle on the valves. The car also had a boot stretched over the back seat for reasons I never understood; hanging from the rearview mirror, as was the custom, was a pair of angora dice. A previous girl friend named Solange, who was famous throughout Beverly Hills High School for having no pigment in her right eyebrow, had knitted them for him. Buster and I would ride around town, the two of us seated to the left of the steering wheel. I would shift gears. It was nice.

There was necking. Terrific necking. First in the car, overlooking Los Angeles from what is now the Trousdale Estates. Then on the bed of his parents' cabana at Ocean House. Incredibly wonderful, frustrating necking, I loved it, really, but no further than necking, please don't, please, because there I was absolutely terrified of the general implications of going-a-step-further with a near-dummy and also terrified of his finding out there was next to nothing there (which he knew, of course; he wasn't that dumb).

I broke up with him at one point. I think we were apart for about two weeks. At the end of that time, I drove down to see a friend at a boarding school in Palos Verdes Estates and a disc jockey played "April Love" on the radio four times during the trip. I took it as a sign. I drove straight back to Griffith Park to a golf tournament Buster was playing in (he was the sixth-seeded teen-age golf player in southern California) and presented myself back to him on the green of the 18th hole. It was all very dramatic. That night we went to a drive-in and I let him get his hand under my protuberances and onto my breasts. He really didn't seem to mind at all.

"Do you want to marry my son?" the woman asked me.

"Yes," I said.

I was nineteen years old, a virgin, going with this woman's son, this big strange woman who was married to a Lutheran minister in New Hampshire and pretended she was gentile and had this son, by her first husband, this total fool of a son who ran the hero-sandwich concession at Harvard Business School and whom for one moment one December in New Hampshire I said—as much out of politeness as anything else—that I wanted to marry.

"Fine," she said. "Now, here's what you do. Always make sure you're on top of him so you won't seem so small. My bust is very large, you see, so I always lie on my back to make it look small, but you'll have to be on top most of the time."

I nodded. "Thank you," I said.

"I have a book for you to read," she went on. "Take it with you when you leave. Keep it." She went to the bookshelf, found it, and gave it to me. It was a book on frigidity.

"Thank you," I said.

That is a true story. Everything in this article is a true story, but I feel I have to point out that that story in particular is true. It happened on December 30, 1960. I think about it often. When it first happened, I naturally assumed that the woman's son, my boyfriend, was responsible. I invented a scenario where he had had a little heart-to-heart with his mother and had confessed that his only objection to me was that my breasts were small; his mother then took it upon herself to help out. Now I think I was wrong about the incident. The mother was acting on her own, I think: that was her way of being cruel and competitive under the guise of being helpful and maternal. You have small breasts, she was saying; therefore you will never make him as happy as I have. Or you have small breasts; therefore you will doubtless have sexual problems. Or you have small breasts; therefore you are less woman than I am. She was, as it happens, only the first of what seems to me to be a never-ending string of women who have made competitive remarks to me about breast size. "I would love to wear a dress like that," my friend Emily says to me, "but my bust is too big." Like that. Why do women say these things to me? Do I attract these remarks the way other women attract married men or alcoholics or homosexuals? This summer, for example. I am at a party in East Hampton and I am introduced to a woman from Washington. She is a minor celebrity, very pretty and Southern and blond and outspoken, and I am flattered because she has read something I have written. We are talking animatedly, we have been talking no more than five minutes, when a man comes up to join us. "Look at the two of us," the woman says to the man, indicating me and her. "The two of us together couldn't fill an A cup." Why does she say that? It isn't even true, dammit, so why? Is she even more addled than I am on this subject? Does she honestly believe there is something wrong with her size breasts, which, it seems to me, now that I look hard at them, are just right? Do I unconsciously bring out competitiveness in women? In that form? What did I do to deserve it?

As for men.

There were men who minded and let me know that they minded. There were men who did not mind. In any case, *I* always minded.

And even now, now that I have been countlessly reassured that my figure is a good one, now that I am grown-up enough to understand that most of my feelings have very little to do with the reality of my shape, I am nonetheless obsessed by breasts. I cannot help it. I grew up in the terrible fifties—with rigid stereotypical sex roles, the insistence that men be men and dress like men and women be women and dress like women, the intolerance of androgyny—and I cannot shake it, cannot shake my feelings of inadequacy. Well, that time is gone, right? All those exaggerated examples of breast worship are gone, right? Those women were freaks, right?

I know all that. And yet here I am, stuck with the psychological remains of it all, stuck with my own peculiar version of breast worship. You probably think I am crazy to go on like this: here I have set out to write a confession that is meant to hit you with the shock of recognition, and instead you are sitting there thinking I am thoroughly warped. Well, what can I tell you? If I had had them, I would have been a completely different person. I honestly believe that.

After I went into therapy, a process that made it possible for me to tell total strangers at cocktail parties that breasts were the hang-up of my life, I was often told that I was insane to have been bothered by my condition. I was also frequently told, by close friends, that I was extremely boring on the subject. And my girl friends, the ones with nice big breasts, would go on endlessly about how their lives had been far more miserable than mine. Their bra straps were snapped in class. They couldn't sleep on their stomachs. They were stared at whenever the word "mountain" cropped up in geography. And *Evangeline*, good God what they went through every time someone had to stand up and recite the Prologue to Longfellow's *Evangeline:* "...stand like druids of eld... / With beards that rest on their bosoms." It was much worse for them, they tell me. They had a terrible time of it, they assure me. I don't know how lucky I was, they say.

I have thought about their remarks, tried to put myself in their place, considered their point of view. I think they are full of shit.

May, 1972

FANTASIES

ONE of the trump cards that men who are threatened by women's liberation are always dredging up is the question of whether there is sex after liberation. I have heard at least five or six experts or writers or spokesmen or some such stand up at various meetings and wonder aloud what happens to sex between men and women when the revolution comes. These men are always hooted down by the women present; in fact, I am usually one of the women present hooting them down, sniggering snide remarks to whoever is next to me like well-we-certainly-know-how-sure-of-*he*-is. This fall, at the *Playboy* Writers' Convocation, an author named Morton Hunt uttered the magic words at a panel on The Future of Sex, and even in that room, full of male chauvinism and *Playboy* philosophers, the animosity against him was audible.

I spend a great deal of my energy these days trying to fit feminism into marriage, or vice versa—I'm never sure which way the priorities lie; it depends on my mood—but as truly committed as I am to the movement and as violent as I have become toward people who knock it, I think it is unfair to dismiss these men. They deserve some kind of answer. Okay. The answer is, nobody knows what happens to sex after liberation. It's a big mystery. And now that I have gotten that out of the way, I can go on to what really interests and puzzles me about sex and liberation—which is that it is difficult for me to see how sexual behavior and relations between the sexes can change at all unless our sexual fantasies change. So many of the conscious and unconscious ways men and women treat each other have to do with romantic and sexual fantasies that are deeply ingrained, not just in society but in literature. The movement may manage to clean up the mess in society, but I don't know whether it can ever clean up the mess in our minds.

I am somewhat liberated by current standards, but I have in my head this dreadful unliberated sex fantasy. One of the women in my consciousness-raising group is always referring to her "rich fantasy life," by which I suppose she means that in her fantasies she makes it in costume, or in exotic places, or with luminaries like Mao Tse-tung in a large bowl of warm Wheatena. My fantasy life is unfortunately nowhere near that interesting.

Several years ago, I went to interview photographer Philippe Halsman, whose notable achievements include a charming book containing photographs of celebrities jumping. The jumps are quite revealing in a predictable sort of way—Richard Nixon with his rigid, constricted jump, the Duke and Duchess of Windsor in a deeply dependent jump. And so forth. In the course of the interview, Halsman asked me if I wanted to jump for him; seeing it as a way to avoid possibly years of psychoanalysis, I agreed. I did what I thought was my quintessential jump. "Do it again," said Halsman. I did, attempting to duplicate exactly what I had done before. "Again," he said, and I did. "Well," said Halsman, "I can see from your jump that you are a very determined, ambitious, directed person, but you will never write a novel." "Why is that?" I asked. "Because you have only one jump in you," he said.

At the time, I thought that was really unfair—I had, after all, thought he wanted to see the *same* jump, not a different one every time; but I see now that he was exactly right. I have only one jump in me. I see this more and more every day. I am no longer interested in thirty-one flavors; I stick with English toffee. More to the point, I have had the same sex fantasy, with truly minor variations, since I was about eleven years old. It is really a little weird to be stuck with something so crucially important for so long; I have managed to rid myself of all the other accouterments of being eleven—I have pimples more or less under control, I can walk fairly capably in high heels—but I find myself with this appalling fantasy that has burrowed in and has absolutely nothing to do with my life.

I have never told anyone the exact details of my particular sex fantasy: it is my only secret and I am not going to divulge it here. I once told *almost* all of it to my former therapist; he died last year, and when I saw his obituary I felt a great sense of relief: the only person in the world who almost knew how crazy I am was gone and I was safe. Anyway, without giving away any of the juicy parts, I can tell you that in its broad outlines it has largely to do with being dominated by faceless males who rip my clothes off. That's just about all they have to do. Stare at me in this faceless way, go mad with desire, and rip my clothes off. It's terrific. In my sex fantasy, nobody ever loves me for my mind.

The fantasy of rape—of which mine is in a kind of pre-pubescent sub-category—is common enough among women and (in mirror image) among men. And what I don't understand is that with so many of us stuck with these clichéd feminine/masculine, submissive/dominant, masochistic/sadistic fantasies, how are we ever going to adjust fully to the less thrilling but more desirable reality of equality? A few months ago, someone named B. Lyman Stewart, a urologist at Cedars of Lebanon Hospital in Los Angeles, attributed the rising frequency of impotence among his male patients to the women's movement, which he called an effort to dominate men. The movement is nothing of the kind; but it and a variety of other events in society have certainly brought about a change in the way women behave in bed. A young man who grows up expecting to dominate sexually is bound to be somewhat startled by a young woman who wants sex as much as he does, and multi-orgasmic sex at that. By the same token, I suspect that a great deal of the difficulty women report in achieving orgasm is traceable—sadly—to the possibility that a man who is a tender fellow with implicit capabilities for impotence hardly fits into classic fantasies of big brutes with implicit capabilities for violence. A close friend who has the worst marriage I know—her husband beats her up regularly—reports that her sex life is wonderful. I am hardly suggesting that women ask their men to beat them—nor am I advocating the course apparently preferred by one of the most prominent members of the women's movement, who makes it mainly with blue-collar workers and semiliterates. But I wonder how we will ever break free from all the nonsense we grew up with; I wonder if our fantasies can ever catch up to what we all want for our lives.

It is possible, through sheer willpower, to stop having unhealthy sex fantasies. I have several friends who did just that. "What do you have instead?" I asked. "Nothing," they replied. Well, I don't know. I'm not at all sure I wouldn't rather have an unhealthy sex fantasy than no sex fantasy at all. But my real question is whether it is possible, having discarded the fantasy, to discard the thinking and expectations it represents. In my case, I'm afraid it wouldn't be. I have no desire to be dominated. Honestly I don't. And yet I find myself becoming angry when I'm not. My husband has trouble hailing a cab or flagging a waiter, and suddenly I feel a kind of rage; ball-breaking anger rises to my T-zone. I wish he were better at hailing taxis than I am; on the other hand, I realize that expectation is culturally conditioned, utterly foolish, has nothing to do with anything, is exactly the kind of thinking that ought to be got rid of in our society; on still another hand, having that insight into my reaction does not seem to calm my irritation.

My husband is fond of reminding me of the story of Moses, who kept the Israelites in the desert for forty years because he knew a slave generation could not found a new free society. The comparison with the women's movement is extremely apt, I think; I doubt that it will ever be possible for the women of my generation to escape from our own particular slave mentality. For the next generation, life may indeed be freer. After all, if society changes, the fantasies will change; where women are truly equal, where their status has nothing to do with whom they marry, when the issues of masculine/feminine cease to exist, some of this absurd reliance on role playing will be eliminated. But not all of it. Because even after the revolution, we will be left with all the literature. "What will happen to the literature?" Helen Dudar of the *New York Post* once asked Ti-Grace Atkinson. "What does it matter what happens?" Ms. Atkinson replied. But it does. You are what you eat. After liberation, we will still have to reckon with the Sleeping Beauty and Cinderella. Granted there will also be a new batch of fairy tales about princesses who refuse to have ladies-in-waiting because it is exploitative of the lower classes—but that sounds awfully tedious, doesn't it? Short of a mass book burning, which no one wants, things may well go on as they are now: women pulled between the intellectual attraction of liberation and the emotional, psychological, and cultural mishmash it's hard to escape growing up with; men trying to cope with these two extremes, and with their own ambivalence besides. It's not much fun this way, but at least it's not boring.

July, 1972

ON NEVER HAVING BEEN A PROM QUEEN

THE other night, a friend of mine sat down at the table and informed me that if I was going to write a column about women, I ought to deal straight off with the subject most important to women in all the world. "What is that?" I asked. "Beauty," she said. I must have looked somewhat puzzled— as indeed I was—because she then went into a long and painful opening monologue about how she was losing her looks and I had no idea how terrible it was and that just recently an insensitive gentleman friend had said to her, "Michelle, you used to be such a beauty." I have no idea if this woman is really losing her looks—I have known her only a couple of years, and she looks pretty much the same to me—but she is certainly right in saying that I have no idea of what it is like. One of the few advantages to not being beautiful is that one usually gets better-looking as one gets older; I am, in fact, at this very moment gaining my looks. But what interested me about my response to my friend was that rather than feeling empathy for her—and I like to think I am fairly good at feeling empathy—I felt nothing. I like her very much, respect her, even believe she believes she is losing her looks, recognize her pain, but I just couldn't get into it.

Only a few days later, a book called *Memoirs of an Ex-Prom Queen*, by Alix Kates Shulman (Knopf), arrived in the mail. Shulman, according to the jacket flap, had written a "bitterly funny" book about "being female in America." I would like to read such a book. I would like to write such a book. As it turns out, however, Alix Shulman hasn't. What she has written is a book about the anguish and difficulty of being beautiful. And I realized, midway through the novel, that if there is anything more boring to me than the problems of big-busted women, it is the problems of beautiful women.

"They say it's worse to be ugly," Shulman writes. "I think it must only be different. If you're pretty, you are subject to one set of assaults; if you're plain you are subject to another. Pretty, you may have more men to choose from, but you have more anxiety too, knowing your looks, which really have nothing to do with you, will disappear. Pretty girls have few friends. Kicked out of mankind in elementary school, and then kicked out of womankind in junior high, pretty girls have a lower birthrate and a higher mortality. It is the beauties like Marilyn Monroe who swallow twenty-five Nembutals on a Saturday night and kill themselves in their thirties."

Now I could take that paragraph one sentence at a time and pick nits (What about the pretty girls who *have* friends? What has Marilyn Monroe's death to do with all this? What does it mean to say that pretty girls have a lower birthrate—that they have fewer children or that there are less of them than there are of us?), but I prefer to say simply that it won't wash. There isn't an ugly girl in America who wouldn't exchange her problems for the problems of being beautiful; I don't believe there's a beautiful girl anywhere who would honestly prefer not to be. "They say it's worse to be ugly," Alix Shulman writes. Yes, they do say that. And they're right. It's also worse to be poor, worse to be orphaned, worse to be fat. Not just *different* from rich, familied, and thin—actually worse. (I am a little puzzled as to why Ms. Shulman uses the words "plain" and "ugly" interchangeably; the difference between plain and ugly is as vast as the one between plain and pretty. As William Raspberry pointed out in a recent Washington *Post* column, ugly women are the most overlooked victims of discrimination in America.)

The point of all this is not about beauty—I hope I have made it clear that I don't know enough about beauty to make a point—but about divisions. I am separated from Alix Shulman and am in fact almost unable to judge her work because she is obsessed with being beautiful and I am obsessed with not being beautiful. We might as well be on separate sides altogether. And what makes me sad about the women's movement in general is my own inability, and that of so many other women, to get across such gulfs, to join hands, to unite on anything.

The women's liberation movement at this point in history makes the American Communist Party of the 1930s look like a monolith. I have been to meetings where the animosity between the gay and straight women was so strong and so unpleasant that I could not bear to be in the room. That is the most dramatic division in the movement, and one that has considerably slowed its forward momentum; but there are so many others. There is acrimony between the single and married women, working women and housewives, childless women and mothers. I have even heard a woman defend her affection for cooking to an incredulous group who believed that to cook at all—much less to like it—was to swallow the worst sort of cultural conditioning. Once I tried to explain to a fellow feminist why I liked wearing makeup; she replied by explaining why she does not. Neither of us understood a word the other said.

Every so often, I turn on the television and see one of the movement leaders being asked some idiot question like, "Isn't the women's movement in favor of all women abandoning their children and going off to work?" (I can hear David Susskind asking it now.) The leader usually replies that the movement isn't in favor of all women doing anything; what the movement is about, she says, is options. She is right, of course. At its best, that is exactly what the movement is about. But it just doesn't work out that way. Because the hardest thing for us to accept is the right to those options. I hear myself saying those words: *What this movement is about is options.* I say it to friends who are frustrated, or housebound, or guilty, or child-laden, and what I am really thinking is, If you really got it together, the option you would choose is mine.

I would like to be able to leap across the gulf that divides me from Alix Shulman. After all, her experience is not totally foreign to me: once I had a date with someone who thought I was beautiful. He talked all night, while I—who spent years developing my conversational ability to compensate for my looks (my life has been spent in compensation)—said nothing. At the end of the evening, he made a pass at me, and I was insulted. So I understand. I recognize that people who are beautiful have problems. But so do people who get upset stomachs from raw onions, and men with blue-orange color blindness, and left-handed persons everywhere. I just can't get into it; what interests me these days tends to have more to do with the problems of women who were not prom queens in high school. I'm sorry about this—my point of view is not fair to Alix Shulman, or to my friend who thinks she is losing her looks, or to me, or to the movement. But that's where it is. I'm working on it. Like all things about liberation, sisterhood is difficult.

August, 1972

THE GIRLS IN THE OFFICE

HAVE not looked at *The Best of Everything* since I first bought it—in paperback—ten years ago, but I have a perverse fondness for it. In case you somehow missed it, *The Best of Everything* was a novel by Rona Jaffe about the lives of four, or was it five, single women in New York; it was pretty good trash, as trash goes, which is not why I am fond of it. I liked it because it seemed to me that it caught perfectly the awful essence of being a single woman in a big city. False pregnancies. Real pregnancies. Abortions. Cads. Dark bars with married men. Rampant masochism. I remember particularly a sequence in the book where one of the girls, rejected by a lover, goes completely bonkers and begins spending all her time spying on him, poking through his garbage for discarded love letters and old potato peelings; ultimately, as I recall, she falls from his fire escape to her death. The story seemed to me only barely exaggerated from what I was seeing around me, and, I am sorry to say, doing myself.

I was, naturally, single when I read the novel, unhappily single, mired in the Dorothy Parker telephone-call syndrome ("Please, God, let him telephone me now. . . . I'll count five hundred by fives, and if he hasn't called me then, I will know God isn't going to help me, ever again. That will be the sign. Five, ten, fifteen . . .") and well aware of its hopeless banality.

It occurred to me as I read *The Best of Everything* that it would be practically impossible to write an accurate novel about the quality of life for single women in New York without writing a B novel, for the simple reason that life for single women in New York *is* a B novel. Even Dorothy Parker's short story about the phone call, horribly accurate—a classic, even—belongs in the pages of *Cosmopolitan* magazine.

I like to think that things have changed since my early years in New York. A lot has happened in the world, clearly. The women's movement, birth-control pills, legalized abortions in New York—life ought to have changed in some way. I want very much to believe this; like many married women, I have managed to romanticize my single years beyond recognition and I spend a lot of time daydreaming about what it would have been like to be single knowing then what I know now—or simply what it would be like to be single again.

In any event, I have just read a book that is enough to make me stop daydreaming for at least a week or two. Actually it's not a good book, or even a book in any real sense, but a series of tape-recorded interviews with fifteen single women who all work in the same New York office (Time-Life, thinly disguised). It is called *The Girls in the Office* (Simon & Schuster) and it has an incredibly old-fashioned, *Best of Everything*, trash epic quality: it is full of dreadful cartoon people who seem straight out of every junky fifties novel—the difference being, of course, that *The Girls in the Office* is nonfiction, real, an honest-to-God case of life imitating trash. Its author, Jack Olsen, has not really written anything; he has instead been content merely to edit the tapes, neaten up the interviews, give them snappy endings, reconstruct them to the point where they seem too pat, too slick, too much, maybe not even true. But they are true, I'm afraid. Bizarre and weird, but true. And because they are, the book, in its sleazy, slapdash, pseudo-sociological way, is fascinating—both for what it says about the women as for the men in their lives.

The women in *The Girls in the Office* range from twenty-four to fifty years old and all of them live alone in Manhattan, surrounded and—as they testify—tormented by exhibitionists, flashers, rapists, muggers, goosers, breathers, feelers, and Peeping Toms. Almost none of them has an executive-level job, and none seems to have ambitions toward anything higher. Their competitiveness is directed solely toward other women; their energies are spent scrambling for little favors and petty advances within the lower realm of the company reserved for women only. That men are responsible for keeping them down does not seem to have occurred to them; in any case, they are not interested in getting up from under. What they are looking for is a husband. In the meantime, they want not a better slot but a comfortable niche, the warm feeling of working in a nice, big, air-conditioned, wall-to-wall carpeted office full of friendly faces and office parties. The office becomes their world, the employees their surrogate family. As one of the women explains: "[We're] producing a product in close conjunction with brilliant men, just as married couples produce children." The men—most of them married—dominate it all, flirt with them, date them, seduce them, string them along, and manage to convince them that all of it is worth it to spend time with such extraordinary creatures. "You have to learn quickly that the super-talented, super-creative geniuses in our company are different from other men," says one of the women in the book. Says another: "The hotshots at The Company [are] so glamorous. How could I get interested in a fifth assistant teller at a bank in the Bronx, when the man in the next cubicle at the office has just got back from Hong Kong?"

The parade of married men who traipse through these women's apartments turns their lives into parodies of *Back Street*. The women wait, year after year, for the men to leave their wives. They never do. Year after year of one or two nights a week, furtive lunches, nooners at midtown hotels, tacky confrontations with their wives. Even the girls who manage to avoid the married men make a mess of their lives. A few become tough in a way that is simply inhumane: "I learned how to turn the men's lust against them. I'd pretend to be interested in one of them and I'd get him to talk to me for three hours and let him think he was making a great successful pass, and then I'd turn around and leave!" The rest manage to come up with relationships with single men that are quite as demeaning and unhealthy as those with married men. One woman Olsen calls Jayne Gouldtharpe has an affair for a year with an insurance man whose idea of rebellion is to throw egg yolks at the wall. After a year or so of what Nichols and May used to call proximity but no relating, he comes over for dinner one night. "We were taking a shower together," Jayne recalls, "and he said, 'You know, all we ever talk about is you. I have problems too. . . .'

"'What do you mean?'

"'Well, I'm going to Italy tomorrow for a long visit, and my big problem is how to tell you that this is the last time we'll ever be together.'"

After two days of misery, Jayne takes a week off from work, flies to Rome with no idea of where her lover is staying, and spends seven days looking for him. She returns to New York, only to find that he had never intended to go to Italy in the first place. "He was a sadist dealing with a masochist," she concludes, "and the ultimate bit of sadism was to stand in my shower naked and tell me that we were through."

There is another woman in the book Olsen calls Gloria Rolstin, who falls in love with an executive named Tom Lantini. (Names are not Olsen's strong point.) Lantini is divorced and lives with his invalid mother in a town house downtown. Within a few months, he has moved Gloria in as an ersatz nurse's aide; she changes his mother's clothes, takes her to the bathroom, cleans up after her, feeds her medicine, plays honeymoon bridge—"And the old lady barely able to tell what was trump!" All the while, she sleeps alone on a couch downstairs while Tom and his mother sleep in adjoining bedrooms above.

The affair between Gloria and Tom, such as it is, lasts seven years, the last three or four punctuated by a long series of physical brawls—"He cut my nose. I sprained his wrist. He blackened my eye. I pulled out about five square inches of his curls. . . . He smashed me so hard on the side of my head that he knocked me down, and my ear was ripped open from his ring. . . ." And so forth. The acts of violence become so commonplace in this book that at one point, when one Vanessa Van Durant is locked in her apartment by her boyfriend and beaten and buggered for two weeks, I found myself shrugging and thinking, Ah, yes, the old lock-her-in-the-apartment-and-beat-her-and-bugger-her routine. What is most frightening about all these fights is not just their frequency but that the women accept it as a matter of course, and even blame themselves for it. "I'll get a little pushy or a little whiny," one explains, "and a man will haul off and smack me. It's usually my own fault." I'm a masochist, he's a sadist; I drove him to it; it's as simple as that. It is, of course, nowhere near as simple as that. I don't pretend to be able to provide an answer as to why these women put up with what they do, but some of it has to do with a society structured in such a way as to make women believe that to be with a man—any man, on whatever terms—is better than being alone. Only one of the women sees the women's movement as providing any relevance to her situation. The rest want nothing to do with it. Says one: "I endorse the economic side of Women's Lib completely, but I don't go around marching or burning my bra, because I think things like that only tend to emasculate men, and the New York male has already been emasculated beyond recognition."

The men in this book are in every way as pathetic as the women they victimize. I could give example after example. There is a chronically impotent married man who attempts to seduce several of the women in this book and always insists the problem has merely to do with too much liquor. ("Foreplay is fine for about an hour," says one of the women who becomes involved with him, "but when it goes on for a month, that's a pretty good sign something's very wrong.") There is an executive, Peter-principled into a job he cannot handle, who hangs on and spends his time whacking off while dictating letters to his secretary. There is another man who becomes so disturbed when his girl breaks off their affair that he sends her a hot-pepper explosive in the mail, telephones her all night and hangs up, substitutes Drano for salt in her salt shakers, and slips a vial of acid into her loafers which burns her toes.

One of the themes the women return to frequently in *The Girls in the Office* is their belief that men are just little boys, infants with "hang-ups in their brains like spider webs." I have heard this theme song so many times from so many women; and every time I hear it, I recoil. It is, quite obviously, a profoundly anti-male remark; it is also, I'm afraid, partly true. Saying it's so gets us nowhere, though. The unhappy corollary to the fact that a lot of men are just little boys is the fact that so many women put up with it—cater to it, in fact, mother them, bolster their egos by subjugating their own—and feed right into the real problem, which is not that men are little boys but that men don't like women very much, can't deal with their demands, their sexuality, their equality. The role of a corporation like Time-Life in this—which underlines the pattern by delivering to each male employee a secretary or researcher he can dominate—would make an interesting book. The lives of fifteen single women in New York would also make an interesting book someday. This one isn't it.

September, 1972

REUNION

A **BOY** and a girl are taking a shower together in the bathroom. How to explain the significance of it? It is a Friday night in June, the first night of the tenth reunion of the Class of 1962 of Wellesley College, and a member of my class has just returned from the bathroom with the news. A boy and a girl are taking a shower together. No one can believe it. Ten years and look at the changes. Ten years ago, we were allowed men in the rooms on Sunday afternoons only, on the condition the door be left fourteen inches ajar. One Sunday during my freshman year, a girl in my dormitory went into her room with a date and not only closed the door but put a sock on it. (The sock—I feel silly remembering nonsense like this, but I do—was a Wellesley signal meaning "Do Not Disturb.") Three hours later, she and the boy emerged and she was wearing a different outfit. No one could believe it. We were that young. Today boys on exchange programs from MIT and Dartmouth live alongside the girls, the dormitory doors lock, and some of the women in my class—as you can see from the following excerpt from one letter to our tenth-reunion record book—have been through some changes themselves:

"In the past five years I have (1) had two children and two

abortions, (2) moved seriously into politics, working up to more responsible positions on bigger campaigns, (3) surrendered myself to what I finally acknowledged was my lifework—the women's revolution, (4) left my husband and children to seek my fortune and on the way (5) fallen desperately, madly, totally in love with a beautiful man and am sharing a life with him in Cambridge near Harvard Square where we're completely incredibly happy doing the work we love and having amazing life adventures."

I went back to my reunion at Wellesley to write about it. I'm doing a column, that's why I'm going, I said to New York friends who were amazed that I would want anything to do with such an event. I want to see what happened, I said—to my class, to the college. (I didn't say that I wanted my class and the college to see what had happened to me, but that of course was part of it, too.) A few years ago, Wellesley went through a long reappraisal before rejecting coeducation and reaffirming its commitment to educating women; that interested me. Also, I wondered how my class, almost half of which has two or more children, was dealing with what was happening to women today. On Friday evening, when my classmate and I arrived at the dormitory that was our class headquarters, we bumped into two Wellesley juniors. One of them asked straight off if we wanted to see their women's liberation bulletin board. They took us down the corridor to a cork board full of clippings, told us of their battle to have a full-time gynecologist on campus, and suddenly it became important for us to let them know we were not what they thought. We were not those alumnae who came back to Wellesley because it was the best time of their lives; we were not those cardigan-sweatered, Lilly Pulitzered matrons or Junior League members or League of Women Voters volunteers; we were not about to be baited by their bulletin board. We're not Them. I didn't come to reunion because I wanted to. I'm here to write about it. Understand?

Wellesley College has probably the most beautiful campus in the country, more lush and gorgeous than any place I have ever seen. In June, the dogwood and azalea are in bloom around Lake Waban, the ivy spurts new growth onto the collegiate Gothic buildings, the huge maples are obscenely loaded with shade. So idyllic, in the literal sense— an idyll before a rude awakening. There was Wellesley, we were told, and then, later, there would be the real world. The real world was different. "Where, oh where are the staid alumnae?" goes a song Wellesley girls sing, and they answer, "They've gone out from their dreams and theories. Lost, lost in the wide, wide world." At Wellesley we would be allowed to dream and theorize. We would be taken seriously. It would not always be so.

Probably the most insidious influence on the students ten years ago was the one exerted by the class deans. They were a group of elderly spinsters who believed that the only valuable role for Wellesley graduates was to go on to the only life the deans knew anything about—graduate school, scholarship, teaching. There was no value at all placed on achievement in the so-called real world. Success of that sort was suspect; worse than that, it was unserious. Better to be a housewife, my dear, and to take one's place in the community. *Keep a hand in.* This policy was not just implicit but was actually articulated. During my junior year, in a romantic episode that still embarrasses me, I became engaged to a humorless young man whose primary attraction was that he was fourth in his class at Harvard Law School. I went to see my class dean about transferring to Barnard senior year before being married. "Let me give you some advice," she told me. "You have worked so hard at Wellesley. When you marry, take a year off. Devote yourself to your husband and your marriage." I was incredulous. To begin with, I had not worked hard at Wellesley—anyone with my transcript in front of her ought to have been able to see that. But far more important, I had always intended to work after college; my mother was a career woman who had successfully indoctrinated me and my sisters that to be a housewife was to be nothing. Take a year off being a wife? Doing what? I carried the incident around with me for years, repeating it from time to time as positive proof that Wellesley wanted its graduates to be merely housewives. Then, one day, I met a woman who had graduated ten years before me. She had never wanted anything but to be married and have children; she, too, had gone to see this dean before leaving Wellesley and marrying. "Let me give you some advice," the dean told her. "Don't have children right away. Take a year to work." And so I saw. What Wellesley wanted was for us to avoid the extremes, to be instead that thing in the middle. Neither a rabid careerist nor a frantic mamma. That thing in the middle: a trustee. "Life is not all dirty diapers and runny noses," writes Susan Connard Chenoweth in the class record. "I do make it into the real world every week to present a puppet show on ecology called *Give A Hoot, Don't Pollute*." The deans would be proud of Susan. She is on her way. A doer of good works. An example to the community. Above all, a Samaritan.

I never went near the Wellesley College chapel in my four years there, but I am still amazed at the amount of Christian charity that school stuck us all with, a kind of glazed politeness in the face of boredom and stupidity. Tolerance, in the worst sense of the word. Wellesley was not alone in encouraging this for its students, but it always seemed so sad that a school that could have done so much for women put so much energy into the one area women should be educated out of. How marvelous it would have been to go to a women's college that encouraged impoliteness, that rewarded aggression, that encouraged argument. Women by the time they are eighteen are so damaged, so beaten down, so tyrannized out of behaving in all the wonderful outspoken ways unfortunately characterized as masculine; a college committed to them has to take on the burden of repair—of remedial education, really. I'm not just talking about vocational guidance and placement bureaus (which are far more important than anyone at these schools believes) but also about the need to force young women to define themselves before they abdicate the task and become defined by their husbands. *What do you think? What is your opinion?* No one ever asked. We all graduated from Wellesley able to describe everything we had studied—Baroque painting, Hindemith, Jacksonian democracy, Yeats—yet we were never asked what we thought of any of it. *Do you like it? Do you think it is good? Do you know that even if it is good you do not have to like it?* During reunion weekend, at the Saturday-night class supper, we were subjected to an hour of dance by a fourth-rate Boston theatre ensemble which specializes in eighth-rate Grotowski crossed with the worst of *Marat/Sade*. Grunts. Moans. Jumping about imitating lambs. It was absolutely awful. The next day, a classmate with the improbable name of Muffy Kleinfeld asked me what I thought of it. "What did *you* think of it?" I replied. "Well," she said, "I thought their movements were quite expressive and forceful, but I'm not exactly sure what they were trying to do dramatically." *But what did you think of it?*

I am probably babbling a bit here, but I feel a real anger toward Wellesley for blowing it, for being so damned irrelevant. Like many women involved with the movement, I have come full circle in recent years: I used to think that anything exclusively for women (women's pages, women's colleges, women's novels) was a bad idea. Now I am all in favor of it. But when Wellesley decided to remain a women's college, it seemed so pointless to me. Why remain a school for women unless you are prepared to deal with the problems women have in today's society? Why bother? If you are simply going to run a classy liberal-arts college in New England, an ivory tower for $3,900 a year, why not let the men in?

Wellesley *has* changed. Some of the changes are superficial: sex in the dorms, juicy as it is, probably has more to do with the fact that it is 1972 than with real change. On the other hand, there are changes that are almost fundamental. The spinster deans are mostly gone. There is a new president, and she has actually been married. Twice. Many of the hangovers from an earlier era—when Wellesley was totally a school for the rich as opposed to now, when it is only partially so—have been eliminated: sit-down dinners with maids and students waiting on tables; Tree Day, a spring rite complete with tree maidens and tree plantings; the freshman-class banner hunt. Hoop rolling goes on, but this year a feminist senior won and promptly denounced the rite as trivial and sexist. Bible is no longer required. More seniors are applying to law school. "They are not as polite as you were," says history professor Edward Gulick, which sounds promising. Yet another teacher tells me that the students today are more like us than like the class of 1970. The graduation procession is an endless troupe of look-alikes, cookie-cutter perfect faces with long straight hair parted in the middle. Still, there are at least three times as many black faces among them as there were in my time.

And there is the graduation speaker, Eleanor Holmes Norton, a black who is New York City Commissioner of Human Rights. Ten years ago, our speaker was Santha Rama Rau, who bored us mightily with a low-keyed speech on the need to put friendship above love of country. The contrast is quite extraordinary: Norton, an outspoken feminist and mesmerizing public speaker, raises her fist to the class as she speaks. "The question has been asked," she says, "'What is a woman?'

A woman is a person who makes choices. A woman is a dreamer. A woman is a planner. A woman is a maker, and a molder. A woman is a person who makes choices. A woman builds bridges. A woman makes children and makes cars. A woman writes poetry and songs. A woman is a person who makes choices. You cannot even simply become a mother anymore. You must *choose* motherhood. Will you choose change? Can you become its vanguard?" It is a moving speech, full of comparisons between women today and the young blacks of the 1960s; midway through, a Madras-jacketed father, absolutely furious, storms down the aisle, collars his graduating daughter, and drags her off to tell her what he thinks of it. She returns a few minutes later to join her class in a standing ovation.

As for my class, two things are immediately apparent. The housewives, who are openly elated at being sprung from the responsibility of children for a weekend, are nonetheless very defensive about women's liberation and wary of those of us who have made other choices. In the class record book, the most common expression is "women's lib notwithstanding," as in this from Janet Barton Mostafa: "I'm thrilled to find, women's lib to the contrary notwithstanding, that motherhood is a pretty joyful experience. Shakespeare will have to wait in the wings a year or two." *You cannot even simply become a mother anymore. You must* choose *motherhood.* "I steeled myself against coming," one of the housewives said at reunion. "I was sure I was going to have to defend myself." Neither she nor any other housewife will have to defend herself this trip; we are all far too polite. Still, it is interesting that the housewives—not the working mothers or the single or divorced women—are self-conscious. Which brings me to the second trend: the number of women at reunion who are not just divorced but proudly divorced, wearing their new independence as a kind of badge. I cannot imagine that previous Wellesley reunions attracted any divorced women at all.

On Saturday afternoon, our class meets formally. The meeting is conducted by the outgoing class president, B. J. Diener, the developer of Breck One Dandruff Shampoo. She has brought each of us a bottle of the stuff, a gesture some of the class think is in poor taste. I think it is sweet. B.J. is saying that the college ought to do more for its alumnae—hold symposia around the country, provide reading lists on selected subjects, run correspondence courses for graduate-school credits. I find myself involved in a debate about the wisdom of all this—I hadn't meant to get involved, but here I am, with my hand up, about to say that it sounds suspiciously like suburban clubwomen. As it happens, I am sitting in the back with a small group of fellow troublemakers, and we all end up waving our hands and speaking out. "It seems to me," says one, "that all this is in the same spirit of elitism we've tried to get away from since leaving Wellesley." Says another: "Where is the leadership of Wellesley when it comes to graduate-school quotas for women? If Wellesley is going to stand out and be a special place for women, it should be standing up and making a loud noise about it." One thing leads to another, and the Class of 1962 ends up passing a unanimous resolution urging the college to take a position of leadership in the women's movement. It seems a stunning and miraculous victory, and so, giddy, we push on to yet another controversial topic. That morning, graduation exercises had been leafleted by a campus group urging Wellesley to sell its stocks in companies manufacturing products for war; we think the class should support them. President Diener thinks this is a terrible idea, and she musters all her Harvard Business School expertise to suggest instead that we ask the college to vote its shares against company management. Hands are up all over the room. "The whole purpose of Wellesley's investment is to make money," says one woman, "and I for one don't care if they want to invest it in whorehouses." The motion to urge the college to sell its war stocks is defeated 30–8. The eight of us leave together, flushed with the partial success of our troublemaking, and suddenly I feel depressed and silly. We had come back to make a little trouble but, like the senior who won hoop rolling and denounced it, we all tend toward tiny little rebellions, harmless nips at the system. We will never make any real trouble. Wellesley helped see to that.

And the nonsense. My God, the nonsense. At reunion, most of the students are gone and classes are over for the year. All that remains is a huge pile of tradition. Singing on the chapel steps. Fruit punch and tea in the afternoon. Class cheers and class songs. On Sunday morning, the last day of a hopelessly over-scheduled weekend, the reunion classes parade down to the alumnae meeting. Each class carries a felt banner and each woman wears a white dress decorated with some kind of costume insignia, also in class colors. My class is holding plastic umbrellas trimmed with huge bouquets of plastic violets and purple ribbons. The Class of 1957 is waving green feather dusters. Nineteen thirty-two is wearing what look like strawberry shortcakes but turn out to be huge red crowns; 1937 is in chefs' hats and aprons with signs reading, " '37 is alive and cooking!" I am standing on the side, defiant in my non-umbrellaness, as the Class of 1952 comes down the path with red backpacks strapped on; in the midst of them I see a woman I know, a book editor, who is marching with her class but is not wearing a backpack. I start to laugh, because it seems clear to me that we both think we are somehow set apart from all this—she because she is not wearing anything on her back, I because I am taking notes. We are both wrong, of course.

I can pretend that I have come back to Wellesley only because I want to write about it, but I am really here because I still care, I still care about this Mickey Mouse institution; I am foolish enough to think that someday it will do something important for women. That I care at all, that I am here at all, makes me one of Them. I am not exactly like them—I may be a better class of dumb—but we are all dumb. This college is about as meaningful to the educational process in America as a perfume factory is to the national economy. And all of us care, which makes us all idiots for wasting a minute thinking about the place.

October, 1972

IT'S about this mother-of-us-all business.

It is Sunday morning in Miami Beach, the day before the Democratic Convention is to begin, and the National Women's Political Caucus is holding a press conference. The cameras are clicking at Gloria, and Bella has swept in trailed by a vortex of television crews, and there is Betty, off to the side, just slightly out of frame. The cameras will occasionally catch a shoulder of her flowered granny dress or a stray wisp of her chaotic graying hair or one of her hands churning up the air; but it will be accidental, background in a photograph of Gloria, or a photograph of Bella, or a photograph of Gloria and Bella. Betty's eyes are darting back and forth trying to catch someone's attention, anyone's attention. No use. Gloria is speaking, and then Bella, and then Sissy Farenthold from Texas. And finally . . . Betty's lips tighten as she hears the inevitable introduction coming: "Betty Friedan, the mother of us all." That does it. "I'm getting sick and tired of this mother-of-us-all thing," she says. She is absolutely right, of course: in the women's movement, to be called the mother of anything is rarely a compliment. And what it means in this context, make no mistake, is that Betty, having in fact given birth, ought to cut the cord. Bug off. Shut up. At the very least, retire gracefully to the role of senior citizen, professor emeritus. Betty Friedan has no intention of doing anything of the kind. It's her baby, damn it. Her movement. Is she supposed to sit still and let a beautiful thin lady run off with it?

The National Women's Political Caucus (N.W.P.C.) was organized in July, 1971, by a shaky coalition of women's movement leaders. Its purpose was to help women in and into political life, particularly above the envelope-licking level. Just how well the caucus will do in its first national election remains to be seen, but in terms of the Democratic Convention it was wildly successful—so much so, in fact, that by the time the convention was to begin, the N.W.P.C. leaders were undergoing a profound sense of anticlimax. There were 1,121 women delegates, up from 13 percent four years ago to nearly 40 percent. There was a comprehensive and stunning women's plank in the platform; four years ago there was none. There were battles still to be fought at the convention—the South Carolina challenge and the abortion plank—but the first was small potatoes (or so it seemed beforehand) and the second was a guaranteed loser. And so, in a sense, the major function for the N.W.P.C. was to be ornamental—that is, it was simply to be *there*. Making its presence felt. Putting forth the best possible face. Pretending to a unity that did not exist. Above all, putting on a good show: the abortion plank would never carry, a woman would not be nominated as Vice-President this year, but the N.W.P.C. would put on a good show. Nineteen seventy-six, and all that. Punctuating all this would be what at times seemed an absurd emphasis on semantics: committees were run by "spokespersons" and "chairpersons"; phones were never manned but "womanned" and "personned." All this was public relations, not politics. They are two different approaches: the first is genteel, dignified, orderly, goes by the rules, and that was the one the women planned to play. They got an inadvertent baptism in the second primarily because George McGovern crossed them, but also because politics, after all, is the name of the game.

In 1963, Betty Friedan wrote *The Feminine Mystique* and became a national celebrity. She moved from the suburbs to Manhattan, separated from her husband, and began to devote much of her time to public speaking. She was a founder of the N.W.P.C. and of the National Organization for Women (N.O.W.), from whose national board she resigned voluntarily last year. This year she ran and lost as a Chisholm delegate to the convention. Among the high points of her campaign was a press release announcing she would appear in Harlem with a "Traveling Watermelon Feast" to distribute to the natives. In recent months, her influence within the movement has waned to the point that even when she is right (which she is occasionally, though usually for the wrong reasons), no one pays any attention to her. Two weeks before the convention, the N.W.P.C. council met to elect a spokesperson in Miami and chose Gloria Steinem over Friedan. The election was yet another chapter in Friedan's ongoing feud with Steinem—the two barely speak—and by the time Betty arrived in Miami she was furious. "I'm so disgusted with Gloria," she would mutter on her way to an N.W.P.C. meeting. Gloria was selling out the women. Gloria was ripping off the movement. Gloria was a tool of George McGovern. Gloria and Bella were bossing the delegates around. Gloria was part of a racist clique that would not support Shirley Chisholm for Vice-President. And so it went. Every day, Friedan would call N.W.P.C. headquarters at the dingy Betsy Ross Hotel downtown and threaten to call a press conference to expose the caucus; every day, at the meetings the N.W.P.C. held for press and female delegates, movement leaders would watch with a kind of horrified fascination to see what Betty Friedan would do next.

And Gloria. *Sic transit*, etc. Gloria Steinem has in the past year undergone a total metamorphosis, one that makes her critics extremely uncomfortable. Like Jane Fonda, she has become dedicated in a way that is a little frightening and almost awe-inspiring; she is demanding to be taken seriously—and it is the one demand her detractors, who prefer to lump her in with all the other radical-chic beautiful people, cannot bear to grant her. Once the glamour girl, all legs and short skirts and long painted nails, David Webb rings, Pucci, Gucci, you-name-it-she-had-it, once a fixture in gossip columns which linked her to one attractive man after another, she has managed to transform herself almost totally. She now wears Levi's and simple T-shirts—and often the same outfit two days running. The nails are as long as ever, but they are unpolished, and her fingers bare. She has managed to keep whatever private life she still has out of the papers. Most important, she projects a calm, peaceful, subdued quality; her humor is gentle, understated. Every so often, someone suggests that Gloria Steinem is only into the women's movement because it is currently the chic place to be; it always makes me smile, because she is about the only remotely chic thing connected with the movement.

It is probably too easy to go on about the two of them this way: Betty as Wicked Witch of the West, Gloria as Ozma, Glinda, Dorothy—take your pick. To talk this way ignores the subtleties, right? Gloria is not, after all, uninterested in power. And yes, she manages to remain above the feud, but that is partly because, unlike Betty, she has friends who will fight dirty for her. Still, it is hard to come out anywhere but squarely on her side. Betty Friedan, in her thoroughly irrational hatred of Steinem, has ceased caring whether or not the effects of that hatred are good or bad for the women's movement. Her attack on Steinem in the August *McCall's*, which followed the convention by barely a week, quoted Steinem out of context (Steinem's remark, "Marriage is prostitution," was made in the course of a speech on the effects of discrimination in marriage laws) and implied that Gloria was defiantly anti-male, a charge that is, of course, preposterous. I am not criticizing Friedan for discussing the divisions in the movement; nor do I object to her concern about man-haters; if she wants to air all that, it's okay with me. What I do not understand is why—for any but personal reasons—she chooses to discredit Steinem (and Bella Abzug) by tying them in with philosophies they have absolutely nothing to do with.

At a certain point in the convention, every N.W.P.C. meeting began to look and sound the same. Airless, windowless rooms decked with taffeta valances and Miami Beach plaster statuary. Gloria in her jeans and aviator glasses, quoting a female delegate on the gains women have made in political life this year: "It's like pushing marbles through a sieve. It means the sieve will never be the same again." Bella Abzug in her straw hat, bifocals cocked down on her nose, explaining that abortion is too a Constitutional right and belongs in a national platform. "I would like an attorney to advise us on this," says a New York delegate who believes it is a local matter. "One just did," Bella replies. Clancy and Sullivan, two women delegates from Illinois whose credentials are being challenged by the Daley machine, stand and are cheered. Germaine Greer, in overalls, takes notes quietly into a tiny tape recorder. Betty looks unhappy. The South Carolina challenge is discussed: the women want to add seven more delegates to the nine women already serving on the thirty-two-member delegation. "Are these new delegates going to be women or wives?" asks one woman. "Because I'm from Missouri and we filed a challenge and now we have twelve new delegates who turned out to be sisters of, wives, daughters of.... What is the point of having a woman on a delegation who will simply say, 'Honey, how do we vote?'" The microphone breaks down. "Until women control technology," says Gloria, "we will have to be dependent in a situation like this." The days pass, and "Make Policy Not Coffee" buttons are replaced by "Boycott Lettuce" buttons are replaced by "Sissy for Vice-President" buttons. The days pass, and Betty is still somewhat under control.

The task Friedan ultimately busied herself with was a drive to make Shirley Chisholm Vice-President, something Shirley Chisholm had no interest whatsoever in becoming. Friedan began lobbying for this the Friday before the convention began, when she asked the N.W.P.C. to endorse Chisholm for Vice-President; the council decided to hold back from endorsing anyone until it was clear who wanted to run. And meanwhile it would be ready with other women's names; among those that came up were Farenthold, Abzug, Steinem, and Representative Martha Griffiths. Jane Galvin Lewis, a black who was representing Dorothy Height of the National Council of Negro Women at the convention, had suggested Steinem at the meeting. The night Shirley Chisholm was to arrive in Miami, Lewis went up to the Deauville Hotel to welcome her and bumped into Betty Friedan in the lobby.

"What are you doing here?" Friedan asked.

"I'm here to meet Shirley," said Lewis.

"You really play both ends, don't you?" said Friedan.

"Explain that," said Lewis.

"What kind of black are you anyway?"

"What are you talking about?"

"You didn't even want to support Shirley Chisholm," Friedan said, her voice rising. "I heard you. I heard you put up somebody else's name."

"That was after we decided to have a list ready," said Lewis. "Stop screaming at me."

"I'm going to do an exposé," shouted Friedan. "I'm going to expose everyone. If it's the last thing I do, I'm going to do it. I'm going to do it." She turned, walked off to a group of women, and left Jane Lewis standing alone.

"It's like pushing marbles through a sieve," Gloria is saying. Monday, opening day, and the N.W.P.C. is holding a caucus for women delegates to hear the Presidential candidates. Betty has publicly announced her drive to run Chisholm for Vice-President. The ballroom of the Carillon Hotel, packed full of boisterous, exuberant delegates, activists, and press, gives her suggestion a standing ovation; minutes later, it is hissing Chisholm with equal gusto for waffling on the California challenge. I am sitting next to Shirley MacLaine, McGovern's chief adviser on women's issues, and she is explaining to fellow delegate Marlo Thomas that McGovern will abandon the South Carolina challenge if there is any danger of its bringing up the procedural question of what constitutes a majority. McGovern, she is saying, plans to soft-pedal the challenge in his speech here—and here he is now, pushing through another standing ovation, beaming while he is graciously introduced by Liz Carpenter. "We know we wouldn't have been here if it hadn't been for you," she says. "George McGovern didn't talk about reform—he did something about it." The audience is McGovern's. "I am grateful for the introduction that all of you are here because of me," says the candidate rumored to be most in touch with women's issues. "But I really think the credit for that has to go to Adam instead. . . ." He pauses for the laugh and looks genuinely astonished when what he gets instead is a resounding hiss. "Can I recover if I say Adam and Eve?" he asks. Then he goes on to discuss the challenges, beginning with South Carolina. "On that challenge," he says, "you have my full and unequivocal support." Twelve hours later, the women find out that full and unequivocal support from George McGovern is considerably less than that.

"We were screwed," Debbie Leff is saying. Leff is press liaison for the N.W.P.C., and she is putting mildly what the McGovern forces did to the women. Monday night, the caucus, under floor leader Bella Abzug, delivered over 200 non-

McGovern delegate votes on South Carolina—100 more than they had been told were necessary—and then watched, incredulous, as the McGovern staff panicked and pulled back its support. Tuesday night, the fight over the abortion plank—which was referred to as the "human-reproduction plank" because it never once mentioned the word "abortion"—produced the most emotional floor fight of the convention. The McGovern people had been opposed to the plank because they thought it would hurt his candidacy; at the last minute, they produced a right-to-lifer to give a seconding speech, a move they had promised the women they would not make. "Because of that pledge," said Steinem, "we didn't mention butchering women on kitchen tables in our speeches, and then they have a speaker who's saying, 'Next thing you know, they'll be murdering old people.'" Female members of the press lobbied for the plank. Male delegates left their seats to allow women alternates to vote. The movement split over whether to have a roll call or simply a voice vote. At four in the morning, Bella Abzug was screaming at Shirley MacLaine, and Steinem, in tears, was confronting McGovern campaign manager Gary Hart: "You promised us you would not take the low road, you bastards." The roll call on the plank was held largely at Betty Friedan's insistence. She and Martha McKay of North Carolina were the only N.W.P.C. leaders who were willing to take the risk; the rest thought the roll call would be so badly defeated that it would be best to avoid the humiliation. Friedan was in this case right for the wrong reasons: "We have to find out who our enemies are," she said. Incredibly, the plank went down to a thoroughly respectable defeat, 1572.80 against, 1101.37 for.

Thursday. A rumor is circulating that Gloria Steinem is at the Doral Hotel to speak with McGovern. I find her in the lobby. "I didn't see him," she says. "I don't want to see him." She is walking over to the Fontainebleau for a meeting; and on the way out of the Doral, Bob Anson, a former *Time* reporter, who interviewed her for a McGovern profile, says hello.

"At some point I'd like to talk to you about the socks," Gloria says.

"What do you mean?" asks Anson.

"You said in that article that I give him advice about socks and shirts. I don't talk to him about things like that. He listens to men about clothes."

Anson apologizes, claims he had nothing to do with the error, and as we leave the hotel, I suggest to Gloria that such incorrect facts stem from a kind of newsmagazine tidbit madness.

"That's not it," says Gloria. "It's just that if you're a woman, all they can think about your relationship with a politician is that you're either sleeping with him or advising him about clothes." We start walking up Collins Avenue, past lettuce-boycott petitioners and welfare-rights pamphleteers. "It's just so difficult," she says, crying now. I begin babbling—all the pressures on you, no private life, no sleep, no wonder you're upset. "It's not that," says Gloria. "It's just that they won't take us seriously." She wipes at her cheeks with her hand, and begins crying again. "And I'm just tired of being screwed, and being screwed by my friends. By George McGovern, whom I raised half the money for in his first campaign, wrote his speeches. I can see him. I can get in to see him. That's easy. But what would be the point? He just doesn't understand. We went to see him at one point about abortion, and the question of welfare came up. 'Why are you concerned about welfare?' he said. He didn't understand it was a women's issue." She paused. "They won't take us seriously. We're just walking wombs. And the television coverage. Teddy White and Eric Sevareid saying that now that the women are here, next thing there'll be a caucus of left-handed Lithuanians." She is still crying, and I try to offer some reassuring words, something, but everything I say is wrong; I have never cried over anything remotely political in my life, and I honestly have no idea of what to say.

And so Friday, at last, and it is over. Sissy Farenthold has made a triumphant, albeit symbolic, run for the Vice-Presidency and come in second; as a final irony, she was endorsed by Shirley Chisholm. Jean Westwood is the new chairperson of the Democratic National Committee, although she prefers to be called chairman. I am talking to Martha McKay. "I'm fifty-two years old," she is saying. "I've gotten to the point where I choose what I spend time on. Look at the situation in North Carolina. Forty-four percent of the black women who work are domestics. In the eastern part of the state, some are making fifteen dollars a week and totin'. You know what that is? That's taking home roast beef, and that's supposed to make up for the wages. We're talking about bread on the table. We're talking about women who are heads of households who can't get credit. They hook up with a man, he signs the credit agreement, they make the payments, and in the end he owns the house. When things like this are going on in the country, who's got the time to get caught in the rock-crushing at the national level? I'm just so amazed that these gals fight like they do. It's so enervating."

November, 1972

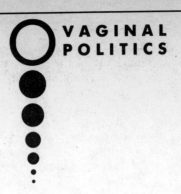

VAGINAL POLITICS

WE have lived through the era when happiness was a warm puppy, and the era when happiness was a dry martini, and now we have come to the era when happiness is "knowing what your uterus looks like." For this slogan, and for what is perhaps the apotheosis of the do-it-yourself movement in America, we have the Los Angeles Self-Help Clinic to thank: this group of women has been sending its emissaries around the country with a large supply of plastic specula for sale and detailed instructions on how women can perform their own gynecological examinations and abortions. Some time ago, two of its representatives were in New York, and Ellen Frankfort, who covers health matters for the *Village Voice*, attended a session. What she saw makes the rest of the women's movement look like a bunch of old biddies at an American Legion Auxiliary cake sale:

"Carol, a woman from the ... Clinic, slipped off her dungarees and underpants, borrowed somebody's coat and stretched it out on a long table, placed herself on top, and, with her legs bent at the knees, inserted a speculum into herself. Once the speculum was in place, her cervix was completely visible and each of the fifty women present took a flashlight and looked inside.

"'Which part is the cervix? The tiny slit in the middle?'

"'No, that's the os. The cervix is the round, doughnut-shaped part.'"

Following the eyewitness internal examination, Carol and her colleague spoke at length about medical ritual and how depersonalizing it is, right down to the drape women are given to cover their bodies; they suggested that women should instead take the drape and fling it to the ground. If the doctor replaces it, they suggest throwing it off again. And if he questions this behavior (and one can only wonder at a doctor who would not), they recommend telling him that California doctors have stopped draping. "And if you're in California, tell him that doctors in New York have stopped this strange custom." The evening ended with a description of the most radical self-help device of all: the period extractor, a syringe-and-tube contraption that allows a woman to remove her menstrual flow, all by herself, in five minutes; if she is pregnant, the embryo is sucked out instead. Color slides were shown: a woman at home, in street clothes, gave herself an early abortion using the device. "I hesitate to use the word 'revolutionary,'" Frankfort wrote of the event, "but no other word seems accurate...."

Ellen Frankfort's report on this session is now reprinted as the opening of her new book, *Vaginal Politics* (Quadrangle Books). When I first read it in the *Voice*, I was shocked and incredulous. At the same time, it seemed obvious that at the rate things were going in the women's movement, within a few months the material would not be surprising at all. Well, it has been over a year since the Los Angeles Self-Help Clinic brought the word to the East, and what they advocate is as shocking and incredible as ever. I mean, it's awfully perplexing that anyone would suggest throwing linens all over an examination room when a simple verbal request would probably do the trick. And when Frankfort informs us, as she does at the end of her book, that "there are several groups of women who get together in New York City and on their dining room tables or couches look at the changes in the cervix," it is hard not to long for the days when an evening with the girls meant bridge.

On the other hand...

On the other hand, the self-help movement and the concern with health issues among women's groups spring from a very real and not at all laughable dissatisfaction with the

American medical establishment, and most particularly with gynecologists. In New York, the women's movement has turned this dissatisfaction to concrete achievement in placing paid women counselors in major abortion clinics and in working to lower rates and change procedures at these clinics; in Boston, the Women's Health Collective has produced a landmark book, *Our Bodies, Our Selves*, a comprehensive compilation of information about how the female body works. But the animosity against doctors has also reached the point where irresponsibility, not to mention hard-core raunchiness, has replaced reason. When Frankfort asked Carol about the possible negative effects of period extraction, her question was taken as a broad-scale attack on feminism. The fact is that if doctors were prescribing equipment as untested as these devices are, equipment which clearly violates natural body functions, the women's health movement would be outraged. It has been justifiably incensed that birth-control pills were mass-marketed after only three years' observation on a mere 132 women. The Los Angeles women are advocating a device that has not been tested at all for at-home use; in hospitals, it has been used safely, but by doctors, and primarily for early abortion. There is a horrifying fanaticism to all this, and it springs not just from the zeal to avoid doctors entirely, but from something far more serious. For some time, various scientists have been attacking women's liberation by insisting that because of menstruation, women are unfit for just about everything several days a month. In a way, the Los Angeles women are supporting this assertion in their use of period extraction for non-abortion purposes; what they are saying, in effect, is, yes, it *is* awful, it is truly a curse, and here is a way to be done with it in five minutes. I am not one of those women who are into "blood and birth and death," to quote Joan Didion's rather extraordinary and puzzling definition of what it means to be female, but I do think that the desire to eliminate the first of these functions springs from a self-hate that is precisely parallel to the male fear of blood that underlies so many primitive taboos toward women.

In any event, the extremist fringe of the self-help movement in no way invalidates the legitimate case women have against gynecologists. These doctors are undoubtedly blamed for a great deal that is not their fault; they are, after all, dealing in reproductive and sexual areas, two of the most sensitive and emotionally charged for women. Still, I have dozens of friends who have been misdiagnosed, mis-medicated, mistreated and misinformed by them, and every week, it seems, I hear a new gynecological atrocity tale. A friend who asks specifically not to be sedated during child-birth is sedated. Another friend who has a simple infection is treated instead for gonorrhea, and develops a serious in-fection as a side effect of the penicillin. Another woman tells of going to see her doctor one month after he has delivered her first child, a deformed baby, born dead. His first ques-tion: "Why haven't you been to see me in two years?" Beyond all this, there are the tales of pure insensitivity to psycho-logical problems, impatience with questions, preachy puri-tanism particularly toward single women, and, for married women, little speeches on the need to reproduce. My usual reaction to these stories is to take a feminist line, blame it all on complicated sexism or simple misogyny. But what Ellen Frankfort has managed to do in *Vaginal Politics*—and what makes her book quite remarkable—is to broaden women's health issues far beyond such narrow analyses. "The mys-tique of the doctor, profound as it is, is not the only negative feature of the present health system," she writes. "Unfor-tunately, the women from the Los Angeles Self-Help Clinic . . . seemed to be focusing mainly on this aspect of the prob-lem while ignoring the need for institutional change. Fem-inist politics cannot be divorced from other political realities, such as health care and safety."

The problems women face with doctors stem not just from their own abysmal lack of knowledge about their bodies, and not just from female conditioning toward male authority figures. (The classic female dependency on the obstetrician, Frankfort notes, transfers at childbirth to dependency on the pediatrician, all this "in perfect mimicry of the depen-dency relationship of marital roles.") They stem also from inequities in the health system and from the way doctors are educated. The brutalizing, impersonal training medical stu-dents receive prepares them perfectly to turn around and treat their patients in exactly the same way: as infants. Writes Frankfort: "We feel hesitant to question their procedures, their fees or their hours, and often we're simply grateful that we're able to see them at all, particularly if they're well recommended." My sister-in-law, who is pregnant, told me the other day that she was afraid to bother her gynecologist with questions for fear of "getting on his wrong side." As Frankfort points out: "The fear that a patient will be punished unless he or she is totally submissive reveals a profound distrust of the people in control of our bodies." (I have, I should point out, exactly the same fears about my lawyer, my accountant, and my maid. Generally speaking, none of us is terribly good at being an employer.)

Vaginal Politics covers a wide range of health subjects: the New York abortion scene, drugs, psychoanalysis, breast cancer, venereal disease, the law, the growth of the consumer health movement in America. At times, the tone is indignant to the point of heavy-handedness. Also, I caught several factual errors. But Frankfort has written with contagious energy and extraordinary vitality; without exaggeration, her book is among the most basic and important written about women's issues, and I hope it will not be overlooked now that the more faddish women's books have had their day.

The tendency in reviewing this book, of course, is to stress the more outlandish and radical aspects of the health movement, but Frankfort's real strength lies in her painstaking accumulation of political incidents. There is the case of Shirley Wheeler, who had an abortion and was convicted for manslaughter under an 1868 Florida law. The condition of her probation: marry the man she lives with, or return to her parents in North Carolina. If she refused, if she, for example, lived instead with a woman, her parole would be rescinded and she would be sent to jail. There are the guidelines for sterilization proposed by the American College of Obstetricians and Gynecologists: no woman can be sterilized unless her age multiplied by the number of children she has borne is 120 or more. Writes Frankfort: "The logic behind this sliding scale of reproductive output has it that in order to earn her right to not have children, a woman must first produce some." For men, under the same guidelines, voluntary sterilization is available to anyone over twenty-one. Period. Another incident in the book, and one that is particularly compelling, is the case of Dr. Joseph Goldzieher, who is at the Southwest Foundation for Research and Education in San Antonio, Texas. Some years ago, Dr. Goldzieher got to wondering whether one reason birth-control pills prevent conception might simply be psychological, and he decided to run a test to see. There were 398 women, most of them Chicanos, coming to the clinic, and one fifth of them were given placebos instead of contraceptives. Within a year, six of the women, all mothers of at least three other children, had given birth. Writes Frankfort: "The ethics of a researcher who considers an unwanted child an unfortunate 'side effect' of an experimenter's curiosity needs no further commentary. However, what should be pointed out . . . is that not only does Dr. Goldzieher work at a research institute where poor nonwhite women are selected for experimentation, but he is also a consultant to several drug companies. In fact, the experiment was sponsored by Syntex, a leading pill manufacturer. . . ."

And so the doctors work for the drug companies and prescribe accordingly, the hospitals take advantage of the poor, the laws are antiquated, it goes on and on. Knowing what your uterus looks like can't hurt, I suppose, and knowing more about your body can only help, but it seems a shame that so much more energy is being directed into this sort of contemplation and so little into changing the political structure. There is a tendency throughout the movement to overindulge in confession, to elevate The Rap to a religious end in itself, to reach a point where self-knowledge dissolves into high-grade narcissism. I know that the pendulum often has to swing a few degrees in the wrong direction before righting itself, but it does get wearing sometimes waiting for the center to catch hold.

December, 1972

BERNICE GERA, FIRST LADY UMPIRE

SOMEWHERE in the back of Bernice Gera's closet, along with her face mask and chest protector and simple spiked shoes, is a plain blue man's suit hanging in a plastic bag. The suit cost $29 off the rack, plus a few dollars for shortening the sleeves and pants legs, but if you ask Bernice Gera a question about that suit—where she bought it, for example, or whether she ever takes it out and looks it over—her eyes widen and then blink, hard, and she explains, very slowly so that you will not fail to understand, that she prefers not to think about the suit, or the shoes, or the shirt and tie she wore with it one summer night last year, when she umpired what was her first and last professional baseball game, a seven-inning event in Geneva, New York, in the New York–Pennsylvania Class A League.

It took four years for Bernice Gera to walk onto that ball field, four years of legal battles for the right to stand in the shadow of an "Enjoy Silver Floss Sauerkraut" sign while the crowd cheered and young girls waved sheets reading "Right On, Bernice!" and the manager of the Geneva Phillies welcomed her to the game. "On behalf of professional baseball," he said, "we say good luck and God bless you in your chosen profession." And the band played and the spotlights shone and all three networks recorded the event. Bernice Gera had become the first woman in the 133-year history of the sport to umpire a professional baseball game.

I should say, at this point, that I am utterly baffled as to why any woman would want to get into professional baseball, much less work as an umpire in it. Once I read an article in *Fact* magazine that claimed that men who were umpires secretly wanted to be mother figures; that level of idiotic analysis is, as far as I am concerned, about what the game and the profession deserve. But beyond that, I cannot understand any woman's wanting to be the first woman to do anything. I read about those who do—there is one in today's newspaper, a woman who is suing the State of Colorado for the right to work on a team digging a tunnel through the Rocky Mountains—and after I get through puzzling at the strange desires people have, awe sets in. I think of the ridicule and abuse that woman will undergo, of the loneliness she will suffer if she gets the job, of the role she will assume as a freak, of the smarmy and inevitable questions that will be raised about her heterosexuality, of the derision and smug satisfaction that will follow if she makes a mistake, or breaks down under pressure, or quits. It is a devastating burden and I could not take it, could not be a pioneer, a Symbol of Something Greater. Once I was the first woman to deposit $500 in a bank that was giving out toasters that day, and I found even that an uncomfortable responsibility. The point of all this, though, is Bernice Gera, and the point of Bernice Gera is that Bernice Gera failed to play out the role. In her first game, she made a mistake. And broke down under pressure. And couldn't take it. And quit. Which was not the way it was supposed to happen: instead, she was supposed to have been tougher and stronger and better than any umpire in baseball and end up a grim stone bust in the Cooperstown Hall of Fame. Bernice Gera turned out to be only human, after all, which is not a luxury pioneers are allowed. At the time, I thought it was all hideously ironic and even a little funny; a few months later, I got to wondering what had really happened and what was happening to Mrs. Gera now, now that she had blown her modest deferred dream.

Bernice Gera lives in a three-room walk-up apartment in Queens. In it there is a candle shaped like a softball, an ashtray shaped like a mitt, a lighter shaped like a bat, a crocheted toaster cover shaped like a doll wearing a baseball cap, an arrangement of dried flowers containing a baseball, powder puffs, and a small statue of Mickey Mouse holding a bat. On the wall is a very large color photograph of Mrs. Gera in uniform holding a face mask, and a few feet away hangs a poem that reads: "Dear God, Last night I did pray/That You would let me in the game today./And if the guys yell and scream,/Please, God, tell them You're the captain of the team." All the available shelf space is crammed with trophies and plaques; there must be forty or fifty of them, some for bowling (she averages 165) but most for baseball, for her career on a women's softball team in Detroit, and for her charity batting exhibitions against people like Roger Maris and Sid Gordon. "I can hit the long ball," she says, and she can, some 350 feet. There is also a framed clipping of an old Ripley's Believe It Or Not, a syndicated feature that has come a long way since the days when it printed items that were remotely unbelievable. "Believe It Or Not," it reads, "A New York City housewife has won 300 large dolls for needy youngsters living at the children's shelter of the Queensboro Society for the Prevention of Cruelty to Children by her skill at throwing a baseball at amusement parks."

Mrs. Gera is a short, slightly chunky woman who wears white socks and loafers; her short blondish-brown hair is curled and lacquered. Around her neck is a gold charm decorated with a bat, mitt, and pearl baseball which she designed and had made up by a local jeweler. Her voice is flat and unanimated, unless, of course, she is talking about baseball: she can describe, exultantly, one of the happiest days of her life, when she had a tooth extracted and was able to stay home from work to see the Pirates win the World Series in 1960. Bernice Gera is, more than anything, a fan, an unabashed, adoring fan, and her obsession with baseball dates back to her childhood, when she played with her older brothers on a sandlot in the Pennsylvania mining town where she was raised. "I have loved, eaten, and lived baseball since I was eight years old," she says. "Put yourself in my shoes. Say you loved baseball. If you love horses, you can be a jockey. If you love golf or swimming, look at Babe Didrikson and Gertrude Ederle. These are great people and they had an ability. I had it with baseball. What could I do? I couldn't play. So you write letters, begging for a job, any job, and you keep this up for years and years. There had to be a way for me. So I decided to take up a trade. I decided to take up umpiring."

In June, 1967, Mrs. Gera enrolled as a student at the National Sports Academy in West Palm Beach, Florida, a school run by an old-timer named Jim Finley for ballplayers and umpires. The Associated Press sent a reporter to cover Mrs. Gera's education, and Finley said she was coming along just fine. "She had the habit of carrying on conversations with the players," said Finley, "but we broke that by giving her push-ups. . . . I had expected a tomboy when she signed up, but Bernice is every bit a girl." A few months after her graduation from the Academy, magna cum laude, Mrs. Gera commented good-naturedly on her experience there. "I didn't have too much trouble," she said. "The chest protector didn't fit very well. Those things aren't made for women. And the players tried to give me a hard time." (Little jokes about Mrs. Gera's chest protector were to become the leit-motiv of her saga.) Years passed before Mrs. Gera confessed that the school had actually been a nightmare. "It was a horrible, lonely experience," she said. "They all thought there was something wrong with me." At night, in the dormitory, the men threw beer cans and bottles at her bedroom door. On the field, the players hazed her, threw extra balls into the game during a play, spit tobacco juice on her shoes, cursed to try to shake her up. She would call a runner safe and he would snarl, "Bad call. I was out." Said Mrs. Gera: "When you begin, you take an awful lot of abuse. They make you, to prepare you for the future. I think they overdid it with me. Tobacco juice. That was unnecessary. It all hinged on whether I could take it. I took it. But after, I'd go home and cry like a baby."

A diploma in umpiring was worth nothing at all when it came to getting a job, and so in 1968 Mrs. Gera began the first of several lawsuits against professional baseball. Her lawyer, who served without fee, was a New York politician named Mario Biaggi, who called press conference after press conference to announce action after action. Finally, in 1969, Mrs. Gera was given a contract by the New York–Pennsylvania Class A League promising her $200 in wages, $300 in expenses, and five cents a mile for a month, beginning with a twilight doubleheader August 1. The sports pages were full of pictures of Mrs. Gera, thumbs up, victorious. But on July 31, the president of the National Association of Professional Baseball Leagues invalidated the contract by refusing to sign it. Mrs. Gera was heartbroken, but she confined her reaction to a string of sports metaphors: "I guess I just can't get to first base.... It's a strikeout but I will come up again. The game is not over."

The lawsuit continued. There was a hearing at the New York State Human Rights Commission, where George Leisure, attorney for the baseball interests, said that Mrs. Gera was publicity mad and that furthermore she did not meet any of the physical requirements for being an umpire. Umpires, he said, should be five feet ten inches tall, and weigh 170 pounds. "Being of the male sex is a bona-fide qualification for being a professional umpire," said Leisure. In November, 1970, the Human Rights Commission held that the National League discriminated not only against women but against men belonging to short ethnic groups and would have to "establish new physical standards which shall have a reasonable relation to the requirements of the duties of an umpire." The League promptly appealed the decision, and the legal process dragged on.

Maury Allen of the *New York Post* went into the locker room of the New York Mets at one point during Mrs. Gera's years in chancery and asked some of the ballplayers how they felt about her. He recorded, in response, a number of attempted witticisms about her chest protector, along with a predictable but nonetheless interesting series of antediluvian remarks. "I read the stories about her and she said that she expected people would call her a 'dumb broad,'" said Jerry Koosman. "Hell, that's the nicest thing people would call her. What do you think she'd hear when a batter hit a line drive off a pitcher's cup?" Said Ron Swoboda: "She'd have fifty guys yelling at her in language she wouldn't believe. If she heard those dirty words and didn't react, then they would have to give her a hormone test."

Bernice Gera waited almost two years for the State Court of Appeals to uphold the Human Rights Commission ruling; finally, in the spring of 1972, she once again signed a contract with the New York–Pennsylvania League. In late June, having allowed to reporters that she was "grateful to God and grateful to baseball," she drove to Geneva, New York, for her début. There was a banquet Thursday night and she was cheered over roast chicken. She was ecstatic. "I was in baseball," Mrs. Gera recalled. "I can't tell you. I was on top of the world. And then, the bubble burst."

On Friday, there was a meeting of the League umpires. "That meeting," Mrs. Gera said. "It was like, if you had a group of people in a room and they just ignored you. How can I express it? They made it obvious they didn't want me. How would you feel? You're supposed to work your signals out with your partner. You're a team. You have to know what he's going to do. But my partner wouldn't talk to me. I sat there for six hours. A lot of other things went on that I don't want to discuss because I'm going to write about it someday. I should have realized if they fought me in court they weren't going to welcome me, but I never thought they would do that to me. That was the only way they could get to me, through the other umpires. If they won't work with you, you can't make it."

Saturday night, when Bernice Gera walked out onto the field in her $29 suit, she had come to a decision. She would leave baseball if her fellow umpire would not tell her his signals. Her partner, a lanky young man named Doug Hartmayer, who was also making his professional début, refused even to acknowledge her presence. But the crowd loved her, applauded her emphatic calls, and was amused by her practically perpetual motion. Then, in the fourth inning, a member of the Auburn Phillies came into second base and Mrs. Gera, in an uncharacteristically unemphatic move, ventured a safe call. Seconds later, she realized he was out in a force play, and brought her fist up. The manager of the Auburn team, Nolan Campbell, who had said before the game that Mrs. Gera was "going to have one heck of a time taking the abuse," ran out onto the field and began to shout and chase after her. She ejected him from the game. Campbell was furious. "She admitted she made a mistake," he said later. "I told her, that's two mistakes. The first one was putting on a uniform."

When the game ended, Bernice Gera, trailed by camera crews and a dozen reporters, strode into the clubhouse and announced, "I've just resigned from baseball." Then she wheeled around, left the field, and burst into tears in the back of a friend's car. NBC's Dick Schaap asked Doug Hartmayer how he felt about her quitting. "I was glad," said

Hartmayer. "Her job wasn't bad except she changed that call at second base, which is a cardinal sin in baseball." As Schaap later noted, "She committed the cardinal sin of baseball—she admitted she made a mistake."

It is hard to believe that things would not have worked out had Bernice Gera hung in there, stayed on, borne up somehow. It is hard to believe, too, that she could not have been helped by some real support from the women's movement. In any event, Mrs. Gera and the movement did not join forces until three weeks after her debacle, when she attended a meeting at the grubby New York headquarters of the National Organization for Women. "I'm happy to be here with all you girls—I mean women," said Mrs. Gera, and plunged into her new rhetoric. She spoke of the "calculated harassment by the sexist operators who control baseball." She hinted at a boycott of the game. She defended changing her call, quoting from the *Baseball Manual*, a publication that seems to provide the messages in fortune cookies: "To right a wrong is honorable. Such an action will win you respect."

"People are saying I'm a quitter, but I'm not," she said, "not after what baseball put me through. Someone else might have quit earlier but I stayed with it. I would have shined a ballplayer's shoes. That's how much I like baseball."

And so it is over, and Bernice Gera has, if not a profession, a title. She is Bernice Gera, First Lady Umpire. That is how she signs autographs and that is how she is identified at the occasional events she is invited to attend. Bernice Gera, First Lady Umpire, modeled at a fashion show at Alexander's department store, along with several other women of achievement. Bernice Gera, First Lady Umpire, umpired a CBS softball game at Grossinger's and was third-base coach for the wives of the Atlanta Braves at an exhibition game. Bernice Gera, First Lady Umpire, sits on a couch in her Queens apartment and looks back on it all. "People say to me, you quit," she said. "I heard some reports back that I closed the door for all women, that I put women's lib back years. How could I close a door? I was the first woman in baseball. What did I do—close doors or open doors?" It is an interesting question, really, but Bernice Gera prefers not to hear the answer or dwell on the past or deal with what actually happened. "I'm in contact with baseball all the time," she says. "Don't count me out. I expect to be in baseball next year."

January, 1973

ON CONSCIOUSNESS-RAISING

TRY to remember exactly what the lie was that I made up to tell friends a year ago, when I joined a consciousness-raising group. They would ask me why I had done it, why I had gotten into something like that—a group, an actual organized activity—and I think what I tended to reply was that I didn't see how I could write about women and the women's movement *without* joining a group. Consciousness-raising, according to all the literature, is fundamental to the women's movement and the feminist experience, blah blah blah; it seemed important to me to find out just what the process was about. I said all this as if I were joining something educational, or something that was going to happen to me, as opposed to something I would actively participate in. The disinterested observer, and all that. As I say, this was a lie. The real reason I joined had to do with my marriage.

At our first meeting, we all went around the room explaining why each of us had come. For all intents and purposes, all eight of us were married—the one exception had been living with a man for several years—and, as it turned out, we were all there because of our marriages. Most of the women said that they hoped the group would help them find ways to make their marriages better. Margo, who was in no better shape than the rest of us but tended to have

faith in theatrical solutions, said that what she was interested
in from the group was mischievous pranks. When we all
looked blank, she explained that what she meant by her
catchy little phrase was devising experiments like putting hot
fudge on your nipples to perk up your sex life. It came
around to me, my turn to explain why I was there. I said
that I, too, hoped that the group would help me find a way
to make my marriage better, but that it was just as likely that
I was looking to the group for help in making it worse.

My consciousness-raising group is still going on. Every
Monday night it meets, somewhere in Greenwich Village,
and it drinks a lot of red wine and eats a lot of cheese. A
friend of mine who is in it tells me that at the last meeting,
each of the women took her turn to explain, in considerable
detail, what she was planning to stuff her Thanksgiving turkey with. I no longer go to the group, for a variety of reasons,
the main one being that I don't think the process works.
Well, let me put that less dogmatically and more explicitly—
this particular group did not work for me. I don't mean that
I wasn't able to attain the exact goal I set for myself: in the
six months I spent in the group, my marriage went through
an incredibly rough period. But that's not what I mean when
I say it didn't work.

I should point out here that consciousness-raising was
never devised for the explicit purpose of saving or wrecking
marriages. It happens to be quite good at the latter, for
reasons I would like to go into further on, but it is intended
to do something broader and more political—"to develop
personal sensitivity to the various levels and forms that the
oppression takes in our daily lives; to build group intimacy
and thus group unity, the foundations of the true internal
democracy; to break down in our heads the barrier between
'private' and 'public' (the 'personal' and the 'political'), in
itself one of the deepest aspects of our oppression." Those
lines are quoted from a mimeographed set of guidelines
which were worked out by the New York Radical Feminists
and which were read at our group's first meeting, along with
a set of rules: each woman must speak from personal experience, the group has no leader, each member takes her
turn going around the circle, no conclusions are to be drawn
until each woman has spoken, no woman is to challenge
another woman's experience. I do not have any idea of what
happens in other groups. It took ours just over two hours

to break every one of the rules, and just over two months to abandon the guidelines altogether.

In the beginning, none of this seemed terribly important. I loved consciousness-raising. Really loved it. The process sets off a kind of emotional rush, almost a high. There is so much confession, so much support, so much apparent sisterhood. At each meeting, we would choose a topic—mothers, success, sex, femininity, and orgasms were a few we took on at the start—and it was really like being part of a novel unfolding, as every week the character of each woman became clearer and more detailed. There were tears. There were what seemed like flashes of insight. There were cast changes: two women dropped out of the group because their husbands insisted they do so; there were two new members. It all seemed heady, and fun, and yes, voyeuristic, and after every meeting I think each of us felt a kind of pride and relief, not the kind you're supposed to feel, some sort of high-principled feminist consciousness or other—we never had that—but the well-I'm-not-as-bad-off-as-I-thought sort of feeling. Women who were making it with their husbands only once or twice a week found there were women who made it with their husbands only once or twice a month. And so forth.

In the autumn, 1972, *American Scholar* there is a panel discussion on women by several notable women writers, followed by a far more interesting commentary by Patricia McLaughlin in which she mentions consciousness-raising. The problem with it, she says, "is that discoveries are made, yes. ('You feel that way? I thought only *I* felt like that.') But what is one to do with them? Discoveries have reverberations. A new idea about oneself or some aspect of one's relation to others unsettles all one's other ideas, even the superficially unrelated ones. No matter how slightly, it shifts one's entire orientation. And somewhere along the line of consequences, it changes one's behavior." All that may well have happened in Patricia McLaughlin's group, but it did not happen in mine. No one's behavior changed; quite the opposite occurred. It almost seemed as if our patterns were reinforced through the group process. The tendency among us was always to side with the woman in the group against her husband, to refuse to see the part both partners usually play in marital problems, to refrain even from asking the woman what *she* might be doing to make things difficult. And as for the discoveries—ah, the discoveries, guaranteed or your money back—even those had very little impact. In a different time or a different place or under different circumstances, things might have worked out exactly as they're supposed to. Three or four years ago, say—it must have been electrifying for women to get together and find, for example, that none of them could deal well with anger, or that few of them were having vaginal orgasms, or whatever. In Dubuque, say—perhaps in places like that, when housewives meet for this sort of thing, discoveries pop faster than corn, and women who have never worked go out and find jobs, women who have never shared household duties refuse to wash the dishes, or some such. Had we been single, say, or completely happy with our marriages... But we were all married, living in New York, in 1972. We had read the movement literature. Almost all of us had careers. We were much too sophisticated—or so we thought—to waste time discussing hard-core movement concepts like "the various levels and forms that the oppression takes in our daily lives." What we wanted to talk about was men.

And so, ultimately, it all settled into a running soap opera, with new episodes on the same theme every week. Barbara and Peter, Episode 13 of the Barbara Is Uninhibited and Peter Is a Drag Show: this week Barbara and Peter went to a party and Barbara pulled down her pants and mooned the guests and Peter was furious. Joanna and Dave, Episode 19 of the Will Joanna Ever Get Dave to Share the Household Duties Show: this week Joanna refused to get out of bed and change the channel and Dave hit her and she threatened to kill herself. Claire and Herbie in the Claire Has Sexual Boredom but Loves Her Husband Show: this week a man in the office Claire has the hots for put his hand on her leg while they were having a drink at P. J. Clarke's, but it was time to go home and feed the children and she never did find out whether it was significant or an accident. And there was also me, with a brand-new episode in my series; and week after week, I felt more and more support from the group and more and more despair about a solution.

A couple of weeks ago, I went to hear Midge Decter speak before the Women's National Book Association. Decter has just published a long, almost unreadable attack on women's liberation and she has been justifiably creamed for it by the critics. The audience at the W.N.B.A. was no more responsive to her, and one of the women in it, in what I suspect was an attempt to make Decter lose even more of her credibility than she already had, asked her what she thought of consciousness-raising. "Consciousness-raising groups are of a piece with a whole cultural pattern that has been growing up," Decter replied. "This pattern begins with the term 'rapping'—which is a process in which people in groups pretend that they are not simply self-absorbed because they are talking to each other." There was a long hiss on that line, but it did not stop Decter. "I personally know of three marriages that broke up because of consciousness-raising," she said.

A year ago, I would have joined the general disdain that greeted that remark. Even now, it kills me to admit that anything Midge Decter says might just possibly be true. But I'm afraid she has a point. Unlike her, I do not consider it a blanket tragedy if a marriage breaks up; several of the marriages I know of that ended after the women entered consciousness-raising would have ended anyway; the break-ups cannot really be laid to the groups, and both parties are better off. On the other hand, it seems unquestionably true that many groups tend to get into marriage counseling, and that the process itself tends to lead to exits rather than solutions. I cannot speak for anyone but myself, but it would have been crazy for my marriage to have ended; and yet, back in June, when I left consciousness-raising, it seemed more than likely.*

I suspect Decter is also on the right track when she links the process with the rap. Consciousness-raising is at the very least supposed to bring about an intimacy, but what it seems instead to bring about are the trappings of intimacy, the illusion of intimacy, a semblance of intimacy. There are incredible confidences traded, emotional moments shared, but it is all done in the context of the rap, the shut-up-it's-my-turn-now-it'll-be-yours-in-a-minute school of discussion. The case of the session on turkey stuffing is too classic an example to resist: no woman ever really wants to know what another woman is stuffing her turkey with; she just wants

---

*I feel that a footnote is called for here, but I'm not exactly sure what to say in it. The marriage *did* end. I don't really want to go into the details of that. But I do want to make the point that when it broke up, it broke up for the right reasons. When it was over, I did not think that I was a victim, or that I-was-perfect-and-he-was-awful, or any of that.

▼

her turn to tell what *she* is planning to do.

What finally happened with my group—and this was, for me, by far the most serious development—was that it became an encounter group. The rules are precise on this point; consciousness-raising is *not* group therapy; there are to be no judgments, no confrontations, no challenges to another woman's experience. But, as I said, all that had begun to crumble by the end of the first meeting, when one of the women in the group was told by three members that her marriage sounded lousy. And I don't want to pretend that I had nothing to do with that—I was one of the three women who told her. As time went on, we all fell into the pattern. We felt free to give advice—and not friendly, gentle advice, the kind that is packed with options; this was more your I-think-you're-crazy-to-stand-for-a-minute-more-of-that kind of advice. What was especially interesting about it—and I gather this is fairly common in encounter groups—is that in spite of all this advice, none of us really wanted any one of us to get better. There was one woman in the group whose sex life was so awful that it made us all feel lucky; I think we would have been quite disturbed if she had shown up, one Monday, having straightened the whole thing out. There was another woman in the group who had what I think is called a problem about hostility. She seemed compelled, at every session, to vent her anger against some member of the group. Both these women were playing definite roles for the group, and someone with training and an understanding of group dynamics might have helped them—and us—by pointing this out. But none of us was equipped to do that, and there were no controls whatsoever on anything that happened at the meetings. I am not sure that even with a leader, encounter therapy works; without a leader, it is dangerous.

In June, when our group disbanded for the summer, I left it and went into therapy again. I am not going to write a tribute to therapy here. All I can say is that I was fortunate, I found a brilliant woman therapist, and at the moment I think that things might work out. At the same time, I don't mean to write a wholesale attack on consciousness-raising. I hear of more and more groups every day, and some I hear about sound wonderful. They seem to follow the rules, they give women a real and new sense of pride, they help them change in important ways, they have to do with feminism and politics and the movement as well as with personal trauma. Mine didn't. My group thought the process could be used for something for which it was never intended. And that is the main point I want to make.

March, 1973

DEALING WITH THE, UH, PROBLEM

LEONARD Lavin simply does not understand what all this
is about.

Leonard Lavin is the kind of man who believes, almost
to the point of religious fervor, in the free-enterprise system. In capitalism. In advertising. In this great land of
ours. When Leonard Lavin sits in his Melrose Park, Illinois,
factory, in the shade of a 75-foot-high can of Alberto VO5
hair spray, he knows that what he surveys is not just good
but positive proof that America works. In less than twenty
years, he has taken Alberto-Culver, a piddling drug company with sales of $300,000 a year, and brought it to its
current yearly volume of $182 million. Leonard Lavin is
proud of this, proud of every bit of it, and one of the
things he is proudest of is the fact that there is a product
on the market, a product that did not exist seven years
ago and probably would not exist today but for him, and
that product is going to gross over $40 million this year.
Forty million dollars a year added on to the gross national
product. Leonard Lavin deserves a medal for that. Right?
And what he is getting instead is flak.

Leonard Lavin simply does not understand.

● ● ●

I will try to keep this from becoming gamy, but it is going to be hard. This is an article about the feminine-hygiene spray, and how it was developed and sold. I will try to keep it witty and charming, but inevitably something is going to sneak in to remind you what this product is really about. This product is really about vaginal odor. There are a lot of advertisements on television for the product that are so sub-tle on this point that some people—maybe not *you*, but some people—might not even know what the product *does*. There are a lot of men who manufacture the product who are so reluctant to talk straight about it that you can spend hours with them and not hear one anatomical phrase. They speak of "the problem." They speak of "the area where the prob-lem exists." They speak of "the need to solve the problem." Every so often, a hard-core word slides into the conversation. Vagina, maybe. Or sometimes, from someone particularly candid or scientific, a vulva or two. But mostly, the discussion of this product from industry spokesmen is vague, elusive, euphemistic. Here, for example, are the words of Larry Fos-ter, a public-relations man for Johnson & Johnson, manu-facturers of Vespré and Naturally Feminine. He is speaking here of feminine-hygiene sprays and cunnilingus; I tell you this for the simple reason that he does not.

"What we're talking about here," said Foster, "is first, sex, and second, that segment of sex and how you react to it. Whether or not one needs something like this..." He paused. "If you were to really get people honest in terms of their reaction, the reaction is not with the product but with deep-seated feelings, not about sex but that segment of sex." Another pause. "In terms of body odor, feminine odor, in terms of that, each man would give you a difference of opinion, ranging from acceptance of it or disdain of it. Some people would consider it a problem. Others would say, 'What the hell's the difference whether you spray or not?' I don't know why I wax eloquent, but I do think everyone's missing the point."

All this vagueness and euphemism is entirely appropriate, of course, since the name of the product itself is a total euphemism. The feminine-hygiene spray is the term coined by the industry for a deodorant for the external genital area (or, more exactly, the external perineal area). The product has been attacked continuously since its introduction in 1966—by women's liberationists, who think it is demeaning to women; by consumerists, who think it is unnecessary; and by medical doctors, who think it is dangerous. In spite of the widely shared belief among these groups that the product is perhaps *the* classic example of a bad idea whose time has come, and in spite of the product's well-publicized involvement in the recent hexachlorophene flap, the feminine-hygiene spray appears to be here to stay. It is currently being manufactured by more than twenty companies (one industry source claims to have seen some forty different brands) and being used by over twenty million women, and this, according to those in the industry, is just the beginning. Says Steve Bray, who is in charge of Pristeen at Warner-Lambert Company: "It will be as common as toothpaste."

In a time when the young are popularly assumed to be, if not the great unwashed, at least free from the older generation's absurd hang-ups about odors, the sprays are selling most briskly to teen-agers and women in their early twenties. "Secretaries and stewardesses," says the clerk at Manhattan's Beekhill Chemists, which cannot keep the products in stock and which has been having a run of late on a corollary product, the raspberry douche called Cupid's Quiver. Secretaries and stewardesses. It figures. Scratch any trend no one you know is into and you will always find secretaries and stewardesses. They are also behind Dr. David Reuben, contemporary cards, *Jonathan Livingston Seagull*, water beds, Cold Duck, Rod McKuen, and Minute Rice.

"American women are pushovers for this product," says Dr. Norman Pleshette, a New York gynecologist. "I think it comes down to menstruation, which many are taught is unclean. There are euphemisms for it, like The Curse. This is something instilled in women from girlhood on." Adds Dr. Sheldon H. Cherry, another New York gynecologist: "It's capitalizing on a small minority of women's fears and sensitivities about odors in this area. The average woman certainly does not need the routine use of a feminine deodorant. And women who do have odors should see a gynecologist to see if there is a pathological cause."

The success of the feminine-hygiene spray provides a fascinating paradox in that its manufacturers have taken advantage of the sexual revolution to sell something that conveys an implicit message that sex—in the natural state, at least—is dirty and smelly. To make matters more complicated, these same manufacturers are oblivious to the paradox: in their eyes, the mere fact that the sprays are being marketed is a breakthrough, a step forward in the realm of sexual freedom, a solid thrust in the never-ending fight against hypocrisy and puritanism. We didn't invent the problem, they say. It has always been there. The feminine-hygiene spray has just come along to save the day. "Somewhere out there," says Jerry Della Femina, whose advertising agency did the campaigns for Feminique, "there is a girl who might be hung up about herself, and one day she goes out and buys Feminique and shoots up with it, and she comes home and that one night she feels more confident and she jumps her husband and for the first time in her life she has an orgasm. If I can feel I was responsible for one more orgasm in the world, I feel I deserve the Nobel Peace Prize."

How Alberto-Culver Tests FDS for Effectiveness (*A Short but Gamy Section*)

A housewife comes to the Institute for Applied Pharmaceutical Research in Yeadon, Pennsylvania, on a Monday morning, at which time she is evaluated by direct olfaction on a scale of eight. What this means, in plain language, is that she simply takes off her clothes, lies down on a bed with a curtain and sheet completely covering the upper half of her body, and a judge takes a nosepiece, places it over her vulvar area, and sniffs. The judge is female, earns up to $1,000 a week, and works also in underarm odor. The housewife is scored: from 0 to 2 means little or no odor; 3–4 denotes a detectable odor though one that is of no concern to the subject; 5–6 is strong odor; and 7–8 is ripe. After the first evaluation, the housewife takes a bath using only soap and water. Six, twelve, and twenty-four hours later, she is sniffed by the judge and evaluated. On Tuesday, the process is repeated. Wednesday and Thursday, she is sprayed with FDS after bathing and the evaluation proceeds. During the four-day period, the housewife sleeps at home but is not allowed to have intercourse. She receives $150 for four days of work. According to the Institute, the test shows that FDS reduces feminine odor more effectively than soap and water—by 74–78 percent after six hours, 53–59 percent after twelve hours, and 38–40 percent after twenty-four hours.

• • •

The first feminine-hygiene spray was a Swiss product called Bidex, which was introduced by Medelline in Europe in the early 1960s. Technologically, the product was a step forward: until that point, all sprays had been the wet, sticky variety; the Swiss were the first to use a propellant called fluorocarbon 12 to produce a warm, dry spray. The American rights to Bidex were purchased by Warner-Lambert, which imported it and put it into a small test market under its original name. At the same time, Leonard Lavin, president of Alberto-Culver, saw Bidex during a 1965 trip through Europe, and he brought the concept back to his company and summoned his chief scientist, John A. Cella. Before coming to Alberto-Culver, Cella was part of the original research team on the birth-control pill at G. D. Searle; once, while working with the raw estrogen used in Enovid, he sprouted a pair of breasts. They were only temporary. Cella is a good-natured man who seems to be thoroughly used to the enthusiasms of his boss; still, he admits that the idea of feminine sprays threw him a little. "We were all a little nonplused about it," he recalled. "Oh, well. They never look to me for marketing decisions. Mr. Lavin came back from Switzerland and said, 'This thing will go. Can we do it?' I said, 'I think we can do it.' We had some background research on this going back to 1963 in the general deodorant field, in terms of what you could deodorize. It was a toiletry, but we were going to treat it as a pharmaceutical—we realized because of the area in which it was to be used it would have to have safety experiments. It is a grooming product, not a pharmaceutical, but it was a breakthrough."

In terms of product development, the feminine-hygiene spray was not a breakthrough at all. It followed right along in the tradition of mouthwashes and underarm deodorants and foot sprays, a tradition Ralph Nader has called the why-wash-it-when-you-can-spray-it ethic. What the manufacturers of all these products have succeeded at over the years, as economist John Kenneth Galbraith points out, is in manufacturing and creating the demand for a product at the same time they manufacture and create the product. In the area of personal grooming, the new product is considerably easier to introduce than in other fields. "Year after year," says Ralph Nader, "in any industry, the sellers become very acute in appealing to those features of a human personality that are easiest to exploit. Everyone knows what they are. It's easiest to exploit a person's sense of fear, a person's sense of being ugly, a person's sense of smelling badly, than it is to exploit a person's appraisal or appreciation of nutrition, and, shall we say, less emotive and more rational consumer value."

The underarm deodorant, which was the first product to capitalize on the American mania for odor suppression, was introduced over a hundred years ago, in 1870. A few years later, Mum, the first trademark brand, came onto the market. It had a primitive formula of wax which was intended to stop perspiration by simply plugging pores. In 1914, Odo-Ro-No, with a base of aluminum chloride, became the first nationally advertised brand, and it was followed by dozens of products containing metal-salts bases, which did control perspiration though they were less successful in controlling odor. The big deodorant boom came in the late 1940s, when the less than euphonious term "B.O." was coined, and in the 1950s, when hexachlorophene came onto the market. This drug, which its manufacturers claim inhibits the growth of microorganisms on skin surfaces and thus prevents odors, was discovered in 1939 by a scientist named Dr. William Gump and became the sole property of the New York-based Givaudan Corporation, which sold it by the trainload to the manufacturers of Dial Soap, pHisoHex (the soap used in hospitals by doctors and nurses before surgery), and a wide variety of deodorant products. In the 1960s, the introduction of the aerosol container clinched hexachlorophene's domination of deodorant formulas for the reason that alternative agents, like aluminum salts, could not be used in metal cans. Right Guard, and other "family-type" products, zoomed to the top of sales charts. At the same time, the mouthwash manufacturers introduced pocket-sized spray atomizers, and the first foot-spray powders came onto the market. The American woman had been convinced to spray her mouth, her underarms, and her feet; the feminine-hygiene spray, at this point, was probably inevitable.

Q: *Miss Provine, why are vaginal deodorant sprays becoming so popular?*
A: *I believe that we're living in a wonderful new era. An era where femininity really counts. And the more feminine you feel,*

the more feminine you'll be. The hygiene sprays are popular because they're an extension of this feeling. It tells me that we've come a long way since the horrible days when women were ashamed of feeling like women.

—Advertisement for Feminique.

Dorothy Provine, in this case, happens to be right. Women *have* come a long way since the horrible days when women were ashamed of feeling like women. To be exact, women have come full circle. Leonard Lavin is fond of reminding his critics that the tradition for the feminine-hygiene spray goes back to Biblical times; he is absolutely accurate; and he is furthermore totally unaware that he is basing his defense of his product on thoroughly primitive practices, purification rites that originated from physiological ignorance and superstition and that were instrumental in the early forms of discrimination against women. Says Rabbi Ira Eisenstein, editor of the *Reconstructionist* magazine: "To take an ancient concept and apply it to a modern one, especially for commercial purposes, to tie it in with exalted notions, is pure exploitation and misleading."

Early purification rites surrounded the menstrual period, which was a mysterious phenomenon: the female of the species was able to bleed without pain, and elaborate religious customs were devised to cope with this incredible happenstance. The most complicated and widespread of these rites followed childbirth. "Women after childbirth," writes J. G. Frazer in *The Golden Bough*, "are more or less tabooed all the world over." Adds the *New Schaff-Herzog Encyclopedia of Religious Knowledge:* "...in childbirth the cause of uncleanness is not the fact of giving birth but the condition resulting which resembles that of the menses."

The assumption that women and their sexual organs are by nature unclean is reflected in widespread practices in primitive societies. Many of these prevailed up to this century and would be quite ludicrous if they were not so barbaric. Delaware Indian girls, for example, were secluded upon their first period, their heads wrapped so they could not see, and were forced to vomit frequently for twelve days; after this, they were bathed, put into fresh clothes, and secluded for two months more; at this point, they were considered clean and marriageable. The Delawares were hardly unique among American Indians: the Pueblos believed a man would

▼

become sick if he touched a menstruating woman, and the Cheyennes painted young girls red at puberty and isolated them for four days. In Morocco, menstruating women were forbidden to enter granaries or handle bees. Many Australian and New Guinea tribes forbade menstruating women to look at cattle or at the sun; one stray glimpse, it was believed, could cause milk stoppage, crop failure, plagues, famine, and total disaster.

The purification rites developed by the early Jews are probably the most commonly known today, largely because they are preserved in the Book of Leviticus. In Biblical times, menstruation was regarded as an impurity (it still is by Orthodox Jews) and women were forbidden to enter the Temple or to have intercourse at any time during menstruation and for a week thereafter. Any person who touched a woman—or even her bed linens—during her menstrual period was also considered unclean. After her period ended, the Jewish woman was required to take a ritual bath, or *mikvah*, and this was also required to cleanse objects considered idolatrous, and men who had masturbated or had had nocturnal emissions. There are Jewish theologians who insist that because men as well as women were required to bathe, the purification rites were not innately discriminatory; however, the status of women in Biblical times can be measured by the childbirth purification ritual in the Book of Leviticus (xii), which holds that a woman who bears a son is unclean for forty days thereafter, whereas a woman who bears a daughter is unclean for sixty-six days.

> *As the party goes on people leave Ann alone. And she doesn't know why. Ann is never at a loss for conversation. It's something else that makes people slowly move away. Something that Norforms could stop right away. What are Norforms? Norforms are the second deodorant—a safe internal deodorant.*
> —Advertisement for Norforms.

Once the basic formula for its feminine-hygiene spray was settled on (almost all the spray formulas contained hexachlorophene as the active deodorizing ingredient, perfume, an emollient, and a propellant), Alberto-Culver's research department, under Dr. Cella, went to work testing the safety of the product. Because the spray was classified by the Food and Drug Administration as a cosmetic, very little testing was actually required: an eye-irritation test, an oral-toxicity test, and a skin-patch test would have been adequate. To its credit, Alberto-Culver went further; as it happens, though, by the standards set by its own chief scientist, it did not go nearly far enough. In an article on deodorants published last year in *American Perfumer & Cosmetics*, Cella itemized the testing he thought was necessary for the sprays, as follows: "Animal skin irritation and sensitization studies, animal vulvar irritation studies, animal vaginal instillation studies using the aerosol concentrates, human repeated insult patch tests on intact and abraded skin, sub-acute and chronic human-use tests, particle size analysis of the spray, and animal inhalation studies." Cella wrote that efficacy tests would also be desirable, but he added, in a sentence that is a masterpiece of scientific writing: "Efficacy testing in this category presents problems of delicacy which do not encumber the underarm counterparts." Prior to its introduction of FDS in late 1966, Alberto-Culver conducted only three of these tests. One proved that FDS did no injury to the labia and vaginas of twenty rats over a three-day period. A second was a skin-patch test on sixty-seven persons. The third was a use test: thirty-one women were given the product to use at home over a five-week period and showed no irritation.

In the meantime, the market-research and advertising departments of Alberto-Culver were at work developing packaging, fragrance, and a name for the spray. "The first piece of research we did in 1966," said Henry Wittemann, vice-president in charge of advertising services, "was a concept test on the product. If you did it today, there would be different results because today the category exists. The first test we commissioned said that the concept was not appealing, and based on that the research agency recommended that we drop the project. But if you looked at the research carefully, there was a suggestion that women weren't telling the interviewers what they really thought. The question came up as to whether women don't really want to talk about this subject to anyone. We had done a questionnaire about deodorants with a concept statement saying that a leading manufacturer of toiletries was planning to come out with a deodorant for the vaginal area. Do you think you need it? Would you use it? When? With a test like this, you're looking for over seventy percent to express interest. If you don't get that, chances are you don't have a product that's appealing to the market. So we decided to go to a research company that had done work in this area, a company that had done questionnaires for feminine-hygiene manufacturers like Kimberly-Clark and Johnson & Johnson. These companies know how to structure questionnaires that deal with that subject to elicit a true response. So we did that, went out with a concept statement and samples, and the interest was over seventy-eight percent. We knew we had a viable concept." Wittemann claims that at no time during this period was the question of sexual attitudes explicitly explored; the product, he claims, was conceived of as a general deodorant, not a sexual enhancer. (Sexually, the sprays are something of a bust: they cannot be used right before intercourse because they tend to cause skin irritation under those circumstances; furthermore, at least one of the sprays causes numbness of the tongue.)

"We considered names like Caresse and Care," Wittemann continued, "all the names that might be in good taste. But every name we thought fit the product belonged to another product. We were using the code name 'FD Number One,' for feminine deodorant Number One. When we were blocked, we just went to the letters 'FSD.' Then it turned out we had to choose 'FDS' because even the letters 'FSD' were taken." One criticism of FDS in recent years has been that its name is so close to F.D.A., a coincidence that might seem to imply government approval. Did that issue ever come up? "Never," Wittemann replied. "The only thing that did come up was an objection by one of our executives, who thought the name sounded too much like FDR."

"I had no idea it would be so controversial," says Leonard Lavin today. "As we developed the product and the research proved to us that there was a need for this product—both from the clinical and consumer viewpoint—we were convinced of what we had. We realized that going to the marketplace with a feminine-hygiene deodorant was not the easiest thing in the world. This was an area, after all, where other products advertised with a certain amount of reluctance. Kotex and Tampax, for example. We leaned over backwards in delicacy, elusiveness, even in design of the package: it was as soft and delicate as possible. If you looked at the first print ads, you would really have to look to find out what the product really did."

FDS was introduced on December 1, 1966. It came in a pale blue and white can, with a lacy white pattern surrounding the label. The drugstore display unit contained a sign, duplicating the first magazine advertisements, that read, "This new product will become as essential to you as your toothbrush." In smaller print: "FDS. The name is FDS. Feminine Hygiene Deodorant Spray. It is new. A most personal sort of deodorant. An external deodorant. Unique in all the world. Essential on special days. Welcome protection against odor—every single day. FDS. For your total freshness."

> *Ten Very Personal Questions*
> *1. Does a woman need more than an underarm deodorant?*
> *Yes. A woman, if she's completely honest about it, realizes her most serious problem isn't under her arms....*
>   —Advertisement for FDS, 1968.

With the exception of Bidex, the Swiss product Warner-Lambert still had in test market in two cities, FDS had the feminine-hygiene-spray field to itself for almost a full year. The drug trade, which is notoriously unadventurous, did not believe there was any chance for the product to succeed. Leonard Lavin, who thrives on the notion of his relatively small company as a little guy plugging away in an industry of giants, believed implicitly in FDS, and he spent hundreds of thousands of dollars animating his belief, advertising in print media, publishing pamphlets for drugstore displays, creating a demand for the product by making women understand how much they needed it. "I don't call it creating guilt," said Lavin. "That's your word. I think of what we did as raising consciousness. That's a less loaded word." There were almost daily battles to be fought: drugstore owners would not stock the item; magazines like *Life*, *McCall's*, and *Seventeen* were reluctant at first to accept ads for it; television had a ban on advertising for all such products. But by late 1967, Alberto-Culver had sold almost $4 million worth of sprays, and Warner-Lambert, a company that could read sales charts as well as any, decided to move ahead. The name Bidex was changed to Pristeen and the product went into a wide test-market pattern prior to national introduction in 1968. "The name Bidex was already taken under trademark," said Guido Battista, associate director in charge of research and development on toiletries and cosmetics at Warner-Lambert. "But I would have objected to it because of the possibility of misusing the product. It might have seemed to have been intended for internal use. Interestingly enough, some of the information that got to the lay people was that these were vaginal sprays, which they're not."

"Our whole approach," said Warner-Lambert's Steve Bray, "was, women have a vaginal-odor problem and here is a product that will solve the problem. They do, you know. And panty hose contribute to it. Women's liberation says that advertising is creating a need that isn't there. They say it's a nice, natural smell. That's their right. But I would go back and ask them, do women have a vaginal-odor problem? I keep going back to the problem. The problem is there."

Exactly how much of a problem American women were aware of before the sprays were introduced is not clear; what is clear is that feminine-hygiene-spray manufacturers cannot be accused of inventing it. In 1968, a market-research firm hired to investigate consumer reaction to the product gathered a group of housewives for a tape-recorded session that is notable for its embarrassment and coyness about the vaginal area. Said one women: "I think the new deodorant sprays are sensational. Not that I have a problem down *there*, but sometimes I think I might." Said another: "I prefer sprays to the foams or powders. . . . The sprays eliminate having to touch yourself."

Says Natalie Shainess, a New York psychoanalyst: "Our society has tended since medieval times, when the odor of the great unwashed was everywhere, to work at eliminating unpleasant aspects of smell. The sense of smell is tied up with paranoia—one of the classic paranoid symptoms is the feeling, 'I smell bad. That's why no one likes me.' The sense of being malodorous is connected with more serious disturbances. These products further paranoid feelings in women and in men about women—and the way they're advertised presents a horrendous image, of women being inherently smelly creatures. It undermines the sense of self and ego even as it's supposed to do something about it."

By 1969, the market for the sprays had grown to $19.3 million and manufacturers were tumbling in. The boom in sales came largely because Alberto-Culver had succeeded in getting the National Association of Broadcasters to change its code and permit the sprays to be advertised on television. (The stations themselves exerted pressure, of course.) The ads were required to be totally bland and unspecific—the word 'vagina' is not allowed on the air—and they were. A woman walked down the beach with her child. Or lit the candles for dinner. Or talked, haltingly, about this some-what mysterious product, she, uh, really liked a lot. Dorothy Provine emerged from what she calls semi-retirement to en-dorse Feminique, and returned to semi-retirement $100,000 richer. The advertising budgets backing the product mush-roomed: in 1970, FDS, which sold somewhere around $13–14 million worth of the $32 million spray market, spent $3.5 million advertising it.

What was printed in magazine and newspaper ads for the sprays was a good deal more blunt than what was on tele-vision. Demure, for instance, offered this: "You don't sleep with Teddy Bears any more." And "Your Teddy Bear loved you no matter what." Feminique's early print ad read: "Now that 'The Pill' has freed you from worry, 'The Spray' will help make all that freedom worthwhile." FDS, in a more subtle ad, nonetheless promised similar sexual rewards: "Being close was never nicer...now is the Age of FDS." Manufacturers who were unwilling to allude to sexuality stressed the importance of including the product as part of the normal deodorant regimen. Said Pristeen, in an ad un-cannily similar to an earlier FDS ad: "Unfortunately, the trickiest deodorant problem a girl has *isn't* under her pretty little arms." Or this, from FDS: "Having a female body doesn't make you feminine. It's the extra things you do—like FDS." And yet another from FDS, this one utilizing the tried-and-true approach to upward mobility: "Could you be the last woman to be using just one deodorant?" Pristeen sought out famous women to write articles about women, with Pristeen advertisements tacked onto the end: Suzy Knickerbocker, Angie Dickinson, Mary Quant, and Judith Crist were among them. (For this, Mrs. Crist, along with Dorothy Provine, was chosen Sweet Pea of the Year by *Es-quire*'s 1971 Dubious Achievement Awards.)

"The reason I did that ad had absolutely nothing to do with Pristeen," said Judith Crist, the film critic. "It was ex-tremely naïve of me and it was two years ago and I'm ashamed to admit I'm that naïve. They were doing a two-page spread that would have eight pictures of me taken by Richard Avedon, with a two-page headline saying 'Today's Woman.' Then I had approximately eight hundred words to write what I wanted to say about women. I decided to write about women in communications. In the final column, there was a cutoff line and about four inches of space, and then it said something like, 'The modern woman who chooses to be immaculate will use Pristeen, a feminine-hygiene deodorant.' It was going to run in eight women's magazines in one month. It boggled the mind. You were reaching a hundred and twenty-five million people, an audience you couldn't reach even if you were a movie for television. Then there were the photographs with Avedon and the negatives were mine if I wanted them—which was the kind of sitting you could never otherwise afford. And then came a huge fee in addition, and I saw my son getting an extra inning in camp, redoing the living room." The fee for the ad was $5,000.

"What did bother me," Mrs. Crist went on, "was the idea of it being a vaginal deodorant. So I consulted some friends. They said, 'Boy are you ever being sexist. If it were Bond Bread, you'd do it. College presidents do commercials for the right Scotch. Why because it is a feminine-hygiene spray—what difference is a mouthwash from a vaginal wash? This is small, unenlightened thinking if we're going to get silly about vaginas.' But the essential thing was, *I* didn't say, in the ad, 'If you want to be a modern woman, use Pristeen.' What I was saying had nothing to do with Pristeen. Well, it was the dumbest decision I've ever made. It was as if I had waltzed out like Dorothy Provine and said, 'Have you used this marvelous vaginal spray?' Which I hadn't. I thought I would get responses about what I had said about women in the media—to hell with the money, the Avedon pictures, *what I said*. Instead, I got tied up with the spray. There were so many gags I could have thrown up. The students in one of my witty classes gave me an enormous box with a can of Pristeen at the bottom. The *Esquire* thing, which was quite embarrassing. Then Rex Reed, feeling betrayed because of my review of *Myra Breckinridge*, retaliated with thorough justification and said, 'Now when she walks down the aisle, people will think, Does She Or Doesn't She.' Which obliged me to retaliate. I got right down to those lower depths, which was the worst part.

"But it was a very educational experience. If Mrs. Gandhi or Golda Meir had posed for a *Playboy* foldout, the results could not have been as bad. It was a learning experience. At my age you don't think you have those."

The first hint from the critics that the sprays might not be merely useless but actually dangerous came in November, 1970, when a Montreal gynecologist named Bernard Davis reported in the *Journal of Obstetrics and Gynecology* that he had treated some twenty to twenty-five patients who had itching, burning sensations in the vulvar area. All of them used the sprays daily. One of the patients, a fourteen-year-old girl, developed "incredibly" swollen labia, and after being treated, the doctor reported, her clitoris and labia remained "peculiarly" abnormal. Davis's letter was answered six months later by Lawrence J. Caruso, a New York gynecologist, who claimed that he had seen many cases of irritation caused by soaps and oils but none whatsoever from the sprays. Caruso conducted a study on twenty-nine of his patients, all of whom used the sprays for six months, and no abnormalities resulted. The study, Caruso said, was conducted "at the request of one manufacturer of a feminine-hygiene-deodorant spray."

The second salvo came in a long, breezily written article in *Medical Aspects of Human Sexuality* in July, 1971. In it, Bernard Kaye, an Illinois gynecologist, announced that "the great American persuader has struck again!" and went on to report that several of his patients who used the sprays had developed vulvitis; the condition did not recur, he reported, when use of the spray was discontinued. "As an added dividend of the female genital cosmetic industry," Kaye concluded, "it is to be expected that physicians will be seeing *male* genital irritations in greater numbers...from exposure to 'Gynacosmetics' [and]...from the use of the masculine version of the 'private deodorant.'"

"Honey," said Bill Blass when asked to explain why his line of cosmetics included a so-called private deodorant, "if there's a part of the human body to exploit you might as well get onto it."

Hygiene sprays for men, which are known in the trade as crotch sprays, were introduced in 1970. They have never been advertised on television and today industry sources estimate that $2 million worth of them are sold a year, 5 percent of the feminine-hygiene-spray market. It is commonly assumed by women's liberationists that products that arrive on the market with the kind of minimal testing that characterized the feminine-hygiene spray would never be sold to men—the assumption here being that men, who are in charge of manufacturing and research within industry, would never exploit their fellowmen as recklessly as they do women. Their argument, however true it may be in the case of the birth-control pill, does not hold where crotch sprays are concerned. Revlon, the leading manufacturer in the men's spray market, has three brands—Braggi's Private Deodorant Spray, Bill Blass's Man's Other Deodorant, and Pub Below the Belt. It put all these products into national marketing with the three tests that are required for cosmetic products sold in spray cans—the eye-irritation, oral-toxicity, and skin-patch tests—plus usage tests. The skin-patch test, according to Dr. Earl W. Brauer, Revlon vice-president in charge of medical affairs, "was not done on the penis but on an area where it can't be tampered with. We do a closed-patch test. The product is kept in place under a closed patch for two days. It's a much higher concentration and we learn much more from such a provocative test." But isn't the skin of the penis different from other skin on the male body? "Yes," said Dr. Brauer. "It's thinner skin and there are more active nerve endings. No patch tests were done on the penis. It's not necessary."

The Food and Drug Administration began looking into the safety of the feminine-hygiene spray on a number of fronts in 1971. It was concerned about the use of the word "hygiene" in connection with the product. There was the general question of the safety of aerosol containers. And there were increasing reports of irritation caused by the sprays. In early 1971, the F.D.A. asked the spray manufacturers for their complaint rates. Four manufacturers replied; their rates ranged from 0 per million packages sold, to 6, which was about standard, to 21 per million. (The product with the highest rate, Johnson & Johnson's Vespré, incidentally, contained over twice as much hexachlorophene as the other sprays. It was reformulated in mid-1971.) Any complaint rate over 5 per million is considered cause for concern by the F.D.A., but it is unlikely that the agency would have moved against the sprays on the mere grounds of effectiveness or excessive irritation. What finally caused it to take action was the increasing weight of evidence against hexachlorophene.

The earliest indication that there might be serious trouble with the drug actually occurred some six years ago at the Shriners Burns Institute in Galveston, Texas. This hospital, which treats severely burned children, opened in the spring of 1966, and in the first six months six of its patients suffered seizures. "We couldn't find any definite reason for it," said Dr. Duane Larson, chief of staff, "so we looked into our procedure, narrowed it down, and decided it might have something to do with the soap solution we were bathing them in—which was three percent hexachlorophene." Laboratory scientists at the Institute took animals—rats, guinea pigs, pigs, and dogs—and burned their backs and then washed them with a 3-percent hexachlorophene solution. Day after day, the hexachlorophene blood levels in the animals rose higher and higher, and they began to exhibit signs of neurological damage. They were irritable. They all dragged their hind legs. "We tested the cerebral spinal fluid," said Larson, "and were able to determine that hexachlorophene was in it, that it had the property of going through the blood/brain barrier. This was important—a number of drugs don't go into the brain but just stay in the bloodstream." When the animals were autopsied, their brains were extremely swollen.

"We found the same thing with the children," said Larson. "As the blood level of hexachlorophene got higher, they would become irritable and have seizures. I remember one boy in particular who had a small burn on one thigh. He was having neurological problems. His serum level was extremely high—far too high for such a small burn. It turned out the nurse was soaking his dressing in a three-percent hexachlorophene solution to get it off.

"We also measured the hexachlorophene levels of doctors and nurses who scrubbed with soap containing hexachlorophene, and in none could we find a significant level. It seems to be all right for adults if you rinse it off. On the other hand, we do know it goes through normal skin as well as burned skin. We had a patient in Michigan—a baby was brought home from the hospital, a normal baby with no skin lesions, and the mother continued bathing the child in the three-percent hexachlorophene solution that was used in the hospital without rinsing it off. The baby had seizures."

Dr. Larson reported on the Institute's experience, and its decision to discontinue the use of hexachlorophene with burn victims, at a meeting of the American Burn Association in the spring of 1967. His findings were picked up by newspapers at the time, but within a few weeks the issue died down. Then, in 1971, three studies appeared that showed exactly what the Shriners Burns Institute had known for years. The most persuasive of the tests proved that newborn monkeys bathed in a 3-percent hexachlorophene solution for ninety days showed brain changes consisting of extreme swelling in the cerebellum, brainstem, and all the parts of the cord. The 3-percent solution was at that time used to bathe newborns at most American hospitals.

In November, 1971, Jack Walden, a public-relations man for the Food and Drug Administration, sat down with a Washington *Post* reporter and told her that the F.D.A. was looking into the dangers of feminine-hygiene sprays in connection with hexachlorophene. An article to that effect subsequently appeared in the *Post*, and Leonard Lavin of Alberto-Culver reacted to it by demanding Walden's resignation. Whether Lavin thought this would make the hexachlorophene problem go away is not certain; what is certain is that until the very end, every company that was directly affected by the F.D.A.'s concern about hexachlorophene looked upon the investigation as an incredible nuisance. Hexachlorophene was perfectly safe. Everyone knew that. No one had died. Thousands of newborns were bathed in it every day in hospital nurseries; as a result, there had been no staphylococcus outbreaks in American hospitals in years. Just because a few monkeys were brain-damaged did not mean that children would be. "We love hexachlorophene," said Alberto-Culver's Dr. Cella. "It's very valuable," said Warner-Lambert's Battista.

Leonard Lavin, for his part, accepted the hexachlorophene business as a small part of his ongoing battle. First there had been the consumerists—or, as he had referred to them in a letter, "negative-minded consumerist groups who would subject our entire economy to a Marxist purge of everything they object to." Now it was the government, interfering in the smooth processes of private industry. It was just like the cyclamate mess a few years back—there, Lavin insisted, was another perfectly harmless product taken off the market prematurely. He Xeroxed a long article by Vermont Royster in the *Wall Street Journal* which claimed that if aspirin were introduced today, the F.D.A. would ban it. He muttered frequently about Ralph Nader, who had been outspoken on the subject of the sprays. "If Ralph Nader had his way," Lavin said, "he would ban Fritos and soft drinks. I heard him say it myself." He commissioned studies to show the safety of hexachlorophene. Experts pored over medical reports about the sprays and jubilantly found errors in them. (One doctor, for example, had claimed in his article to have seen anal infections he traced to the perfume used in scented toilet paper. This was absurd, said Alberto-Culver's Cella: the scent came not from the paper but from the cardboard roll within; the perfume used never came in actual contact with the body.) Gus Kass, a vice-president of Alberto-Culver, delivered a speech in Chicago decrying the attacks on the cosmetics industry by newspapers and magazines. "All of them," said Kass, "are witches' brews of distorted facts, half-truths, or outright falsehoods. . . . What all of the critics fail to understand is that there is no substance to which some person is *not* allergic."

And so it went. There was bound to be some irritation from the feminine-hygiene sprays because there were bound to be some individuals who were allergic to them. And as to the rest of the complaints, the manufacturers said, these had nothing to do with hexachlorophene. Women using the products were simply using them wrong—not holding the spray far enough from their bodies, or spraying just before intercourse, or spraying the actual vaginal area. (There were, to be sure, many reactions to the sprays that were caused by misuse; some manufacturers have recently inserted more explicit instructions in the spray kits.) As for hexachlorophene, most of the sprays contained less than one-tenth of 1 percent—and even if it could be shown that hexachlorophene was dangerous to humans, such a tiny amount would never hurt.

In December, 1971, the F.D.A. took its first action against

hexachlorophene, announcing it was no longer recommending bathing of infants in a 3-percent hexachlorophene solution. A month later, when there was a staph outbreak in a New Haven hospital that had stopped using pHisoHex, the drug industry was as jubilant as it could be under the circumstances. But the F.D.A. claimed that the outbreak could not be traced to the ban and continued to move against the drug. It announced a three-part proposal: hexachlorophene would be banned from cosmetics except when it was used as a preservative; all drugs containing hexachlorophene would be required to carry warnings; and any drug with more than three-quarters of 1 percent hexachlorophene would be sold by prescription only. (Not until seven months later, when thirty-nine French infants died from the external use of a baby powder that contained, through a manufacturing error, 6 percent hexachlorophene, did the F.D.A. make final its over-the-counter ban on the drug.)

Feminine-hygiene-spray manufacturers could have fought the proposal at this point. But since the first reports of F.D.A. concern, sales of the product had dropped off. A January, 1972, attack in *Consumer Reports* had not helped. And so, voluntarily, all the manufacturers removed the drug from the feminine-spray formulas. Alberto-Culver replaced it with another antibacterial agent, and then refused to tell the press what it was. Warner-Lambert removed it entirely (they claimed it was used only as a preservative), and found that Pristeen continued to work exactly as it had before. The industry sat back, quietly, and consoled itself with memories of the cranberry scare. That had blown over ultimately, and this would, too. In the meantime, sales of the product, which had been expected to grow to $53 million in 1971, held firm at the $40 million mark. Still, $40 million worth of product wasn't bad. There were women out there who were loyal, who still wanted to buy. The rest of the public would forget. It always does.

> *Today children in kindergarten are taught the facts of human birth; biology is no longer a taboo subject. But a product that recognizes the existence of the difference between man and woman—and also happens to be relatively new—was sure to become a target in the age of consumerism and women's lib. Soap*

and water were good enough for grandma, but we think women have changed. Our sales and those of our competitors prove it. —From a form letter written by Leonard Lavin to customers requesting information on the safety of feminine-hygiene sprays.

Leonard Lavin simply does not understand what all this is about.

March, 1973

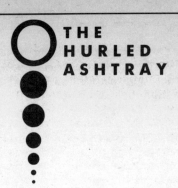

THE HURLED ASHTRAY

I **ONCE** heard a swell story about Gary Cooper. The person I heard the story from did this terrific Gary Cooper imitation, and it may be that when I tell you the story (which I am about to), it will lose something in print. It may lose everything, in fact. But enough. The story was that Gary Cooper was in a London restaurant at a large table of friends. He was sitting in a low chair, with his back to the rest of the room, so no one in the restaurant even knew that he was tall, much less that he was Gary Cooper. Across the way was a group of Teddy boys (this episode took place long long ago, you see), and they were all misbehaving and making nasty remarks about a woman at Cooper's table. Cooper turned around to give them his best mean-and-threatening stare, but they went right on. Finally he got up, very very slowly, so slowly that it took almost a minute for him to go from this short person in a low chair to a ten-foot-tall man with Gary Cooper's head on top of his shoulders. He loped over to the table of Teddy boys, looked down at them, and said, "Wouldja mind sayin' that agin?" The men were utterly cowed and left the restaurant shortly thereafter.

Well, you had to be there.

I thought of Gary Cooper and his way with words the other day. Longingly. Because in the mail, from an editor of *New York* magazine, came an excerpt from a book by Michael Korda called *Male Chauvinism: How It Works* (Random House). I have no idea whether Korda's book is any good at all, but the excerpt was fascinating, a sort of reverse-twist update on Francis Macomber, as well as a pathetic contrast to the Gary Cooper story. It seems that Korda, his wife, and another woman were having dinner in a London restaurant recently. Across the way was a table of drunks doing sensitive things like sniggering and leering and throwing bread balls at Mrs. Korda, who is a looker. Her back was to them, and she refused to acknowledge their presence, instead apparently choosing to let the flying bread balls bounce off her back onto the floor. Then, one of the men sent over a waiter with a silver tray. On it was a printed card, the kind you can buy in novelty shops, which read: "I want to sleep with you! Tick off your favorite love position from the list below, and return this card with your telephone number. . . ." Korda tore up the card before his wife could even see it, and then, consumed with rage, he picked up an ashtray and threw it at the man who had sent the card. A fracas ensued, and before long, Korda, his wife, and their woman friend were out on the street. Mrs. Korda was furious.

"If you ever do that again," she screamed, "I'll leave you! Do you think I couldn't have handled that, or ignored it? Did I ask you to come to my defense against some poor stupid drunk? You didn't even think, you just reacted like a male chauvinist. You leapt up to defend *your* woman, *your* honor, you made me seem cheap and foolish and powerless. . . . God Almighty, can't you see it was none of your business! Can't you understand how it makes me feel? I don't mind being hassled by some drunk, I can take that, but to be treated like a chattel, to be robbed of any right to decide for myself whether I'd been insulted, or how badly, to have you react for me because I'm *your* woman . . . that's really sickening, it's like being a slave." Korda repeats the story (his wife's diatribe is even longer in the original version) and then, in a *mea culpa* that is only too reminiscent of the sort that used to appear in 1960s books by white liberals about blacks, he concludes that his wife is doubtless right, that men do tend to treat women merely as appendages of themselves.

Before printing the article, *New York* asked several couples—including my husband and me—what our reaction was to what happened, and what we would have done under the circumstances. My initial reaction to the entire business was that no one ever sends me notes like that in restaurants. I sent that off to the editor, but a few days later I got to thinking about the story, and it began to seem to me that the episode just might be a distillation of everything that has happened to men and women as a result of the women's movement, and if not that, at least a way to write about etiquette after the revolution, and if not that, nothing at all. Pulled as I was by these three possibilities, I told the story over dinner to four friends and asked for their reaction. The first, a man, said that he thought Mrs. Korda was completely right. The second, a woman, said she thought Korda's behavior was totally understandable. The third, a man, said that both parties had behaved badly. The fourth, my friend Martha, said it was the second most boring thing she had ever heard, the most boring being a story I had just told her about a fight my college roommate had with a cabdriver at Kennedy Airport.

In any case, before any serious discussion of the incident of the hurled ashtray, I would like to raise some questions for which I have no answers. I raise them simply because if that story were fed into a computer, the only possible response it could make is We Do Not Have Sufficient Information To Make An Evaluation. For example:

Do the Kordas have a good marriage?

Was the heat working in their London hotel room the night of the fracas?

Was it raining out?

What did the second woman at the table look like? Was she as pretty as Mrs. Korda? Was she ugly? Was part of Michael Korda's reaction—and his desire to assert possession of his wife—the result of the possibility that he suspected the drunks thought he was with someone funny-looking?

What kind of a tacky restaurant is it where a waiter delivers a dirty message on a silver tray?

What about a woman who ignores flying bread balls? Wasn't her husband justified in thinking she would be no more interested in novelty cards?

Did Michael Korda pay the check before or after throwing the ashtray? Did he tip the standard 15 percent?

Since the incident occurs in London, a city notorious for its rampant homoerotic behavior, and since the table of drunks was all male, isn't it possible that the printed card was in fact intended not for Mrs. Korda but for Michael? In which case how should we now view his response, if at all?

There might be those who would raise questions about the ashtray itself: was it a big, heavy ashtray, these people might ask, or a dinky little round one? Was it glass or was it plastic? These questions are irrelevant.

In the absence of answers to any of the above, I would nonetheless like to offer some random musings. First, I think it is absurd for Mrs. Korda to think that she and she alone was involved in the incident. Yes, it might have been nice had her husband consulted her; and yes, it would have been even nicer had he turned out to be Gary Cooper, or failing that, Dave DeBusschere, or even Howard Cosell—anyone but this suave flinger of ashtrays he turned out to be. But the fact remains that the men at the table *were* insulting Korda, and disturbing his dinner, as well as hers. Their insult was childish and Korda's reaction was ludicrous, but Mrs. Korda matched them all by reducing a complicated and rather interesting emotional situation to a tedious set of movement platitudes.

Beyond that—and the Kordas quite aside, because God Almighty (as Mrs. Korda might put it) knows what it is they are into—I wonder whether there is any response a man could make in that situation which would not disappoint a feminist. Yes, I want to be treated as an equal and not as an appendage or possession or spare rib, but I also want to be taken care of. Isn't any man sitting at a table with someone like me damned whatever he does? If the drunks in question are simply fools, conventioneers with funny paper hats, I suppose that a possible reaction would be utter cool. But if they were truly insulting and disturbing, some response does seem called for. Some wild and permanent gesture of size. But on whose part? And what should it consist of? And how tall do you have to be to bring it off? And where is the point that a mild show of strength becomes crude macho vulgarity; where does reserve veer off into passivity?

Like almost every other question in this column, I have no positive answer. But I think that if I ever found myself in a similar situation, and if it was truly demeaning, I would prefer that my husband handle it. My husband informs me, after some consideration, that the Gary Cooper approach would not work. But he could, for example, call over the captain and complain discreetly, perhaps even ask that our table be moved. He could hire a band of aging Teddy boys to find out where the drunks were staying and short-sheet all their beds. Or—and I think I prefer this—he could produce, from his jacket pocket, a printed card from a novelty shop reading: "I'm terribly sorry, but as you can see by looking at our dinner companion, my wife and I have other plans."

I'm going out to have those cards made up right now.

April, 1973

TRUTH AND CONSEQUENCES

READ something in a reporting piece years ago that made a profound impression on me. The way I remember the incident (which probably has almost nothing to do with what actually happened) is this: a group of pathetically naïve out-of-towners are in New York for a week and want very much to go to Coney Island. They go to Times Square to take the subway, but instead of taking the train to Brooklyn, they take an uptown train to the Bronx. And what knocked me out about that incident was that the reporter involved had been cool enough and detached enough and professional enough and (I could not help thinking) cruel enough to let this hopeless group take the wrong train. I could never have done it. And when I read the article, I was disturbed and sorry that I could not: the story is a whole lot better when they take the wrong train.

When I first read that, I was a newspaper reporter, and I still had some illusions about objectivity—and certainly about that thing that has come to be known as participatory journalism; I believed that reporters had no business getting really involved in what they were writing about. Which did not seem to me to be a problem at the time. A good part of the reason I became a newspaper reporter was that I was much too cynical and detached to become involved in anything; I was temperamentally suited to be a witness to events. Or so I told myself.

And now things have changed. I would still hate to be described as a participatory journalist; but I am a writer and I am a feminist, and the two seem to be constantly in conflict.

The problem, I'm afraid, is that as a writer my commitment is to something that, God help me, I think of as The Truth, and as a feminist my commitment is to the women's movement. And ever since I became loosely involved with it, it has seemed to me one of the recurring ironies of this movement that there is no way to tell the truth about it without, in some small way, seeming to hurt it. The first dim awareness I had of this was during an episode that has become known as the *Ladies' Home Journal* action. A couple of years ago, as you may remember, a group of feminists sat in at the offices of *Journal* editor John Mack Carter to protest the antediluvian editorial content of his magazine; to their shock, Carter acceded to their main demand, and gave them ten pages of their own in the *Journal*, and $10,000. Shortly thereafter, I was asked if I would help "edit" the articles that were being written for the section—I put edit in quotes, because what we were really doing was rewriting them—and I began to sit in on a series of meetings with movement leaders that I found alternatingly fascinating, horrifying, and hilarious. The moment I treasured most occurred when the first draft of the article on sex was read aloud. The article was a conversation by five feminists. The first woman to speak began, I thought, quite reasonably. "I find," she said, "that as I have grown more aware of who I am, I have grown more in touch with my sexuality." The second woman—and you must remember that this was supposed to be a conversation—then said, "I have never had any sensitivity in my vagina." It seemed to me that the only possible remark a third person might contribute was "Coffee, tea, or milk?"— there was no other way to turn it into a sensible exchange. Anyway, when the incident happened, I told it to several friends, who all laughed and loved the story as much as I did. But the difference was that they thought I was telling the story in order to make the movement sound silly, whereas I was telling the story simply in order to describe what was going on.

Years pass, and it is 1972 and I am at the Democratic Convention in Miami attending a rump, half-secret meeting:

a group of Betty Friedan's followers are trying to organize a drive to make Shirley Chisholm Vice-President. Friedan is not here, but Jacqui Ceballos, a leader in N.O.W., *is*, and it is instantly apparent to the journalists in the room that she does not know what she is talking about. It is Monday afternoon and she is telling the group of partisans assembled in this dingy hotel room that petitions supporting Chisholm's Vice-Presidential candidacy must be in at the National Committee by Tuesday afternoon. But the President won't be nominated until Wednesday night; clearly the Vice-Presidential petitions do not have to be filed until the next day. I am supposed to be a reporter here and let things happen. I am supposed to let them take the wrong train. But I can't, and my hand is up, and I am saying that they must be wrong, they must have gotten the wrong information, there's no need to rush the petitions, they can't be due until Thursday. Afterward, I walk out onto Collins Avenue with a fellow journalist/feminist who has managed to keep her mouth shut. "I guess I got a little carried away in there," I say guiltily. "I guess you did," she replies. (The next night, at the convention debate on abortion, there are women reporters so passionately involved in the issue that they are lobbying the delegates. I feel slightly less guilty. But not much.)

To give you another example, a book comes in for review. I am on the list now, The Woman List, and the books come in all the time. Novels by women. Nonfiction books about women and the women's movement. The apparently endless number of movement-oriented and movement-inspired anthologies on feminism; the even more endless number of anthologies on the role of the family or the future of the family or the decline of the family. I take up a book, a book I think might make a column. It is *Women and Madness*, by Phyllis Chesler. I agree with the book politically. What Chesler is saying is that the psychological profession has always applied a double standard when dealing with women; that psychological definitions of madness have been dictated by what men believe women's role ought to be; and this is wrong. Right on, Phyllis. But here is the book: it is badly written and self-indulgent, and the research seems to me to be full of holes. If I say this, though, I will hurt the book politically, provide a way for people who want to dismiss Chesler's conclusions to ignore them entirely. On the other hand, if I fail to say that there are problems with the book, I'm applying a double standard of my own, treating works that are important to the movement differently from others: babying them, tending to gloss over their faults, gentling the author as if she and her book were somehow incapable of withstanding a single carping clause. *Her heart is in the right place; why knock her when there are so many truly evil books around?* This is what is known in the women's movement as sisterhood, and it is good politics, I suppose, but it doesn't make for good criticism. Or honesty. Or the truth. (Furthermore, it is every bit as condescending as the sort of criticism men apply to books about women these days—that unconsciously patronizing tone that treats books by and about women as some sort of sub-genre of literature, outside the mainstream, not quite relevant, interesting really, how-these-women-do-go-on-and-we-really-must-try-to-understand-what-they-are-getting-at-whatever-it-is.)

I will tell you one more story to the point—though this one is not about me. A year and a half ago, some women from the Los Angeles Self-Help Clinic came to New York to demonstrate do-it-yourself gynecology and performed an abortion onstage using a controversial device called the Karman cannula. Subsequently, the woman on whom the abortion had been performed developed a serious infection and had to go into the hospital for a D and C. One of the reporters covering the story, a feminist, found out about the infection, but she decided not to make the fact public, because she thought that to do so might hurt the self-help movement. When I heard about it, I was appalled; I was more appalled when I realized that I understood why she had done it.

But I cannot excuse that kind of self-censorship, either in that reporter or in myself. I think that many of us in this awkward position worry too much about what the movement will think and how what we write will affect the movement. In fact, the movement is nothing more than an amorphous blob of individual women and groups, most of whom disagree with each other. In fact, no amount of criticism of the movement will stop its forward momentum. In fact, I am intelligent enough to know that nothing I write really matters in any significant way to any of it. And knowing all this, I worry. I am a writer. I am a feminist.

When I manage, from time to time, to overcome my political leanings and get at the truth, I feel a little better. And then I worry some more.

May, 1973

BAKING OFF

ROXANNE Frisbie brought her own pan to the twenty-fourth annual Pillsbury Bake-Off. "I feel like a nut," she said. "It's just a plain old dumb pan, but everything I do is in that crazy pan." As it happens, Mrs. Frisbie had no cause whatsoever to feel like a nut: it seemed that at least half the 100 finalists in the Bake-It-Easy Bake-Off had brought something with them—their own sausages, their own pie pans, their own apples. Edna Buckley, who was fresh from representing New York State at the National Chicken Cooking Contest, where her recipe for fried chicken in a batter of beer, cheese, and crushed pretzels had gone down to defeat, brought with her a lucky handkerchief, a lucky horseshoe, a lucky dime for her shoe, a potholder with the Pillsbury Poppin' Fresh Doughboy on it, an Our Blessed Lady pin, and all of her jewelry, including a silver charm also in the shape of the doughboy. Mrs. Frisbie and Mrs. Buckley and the other finalists came to the Bake-Off to bake off for $65,000 in cash prizes; in Mrs. Frisbie's case, this meant making something she created herself and named Butterscotch Crescent Rolls—and which Pillsbury promptly, and to Mrs. Frisbie's dismay, renamed Sweet 'N Creamy Crescent Crisps. Almost all the recipes in the finals were renamed by

Pillsbury using a lot of crispy snicky snacky words. An exception to this was Sharon Schubert's Wiki Wiki Coffee Cake, a name which ought to have been snicky snacky enough; but Pillsbury, in a moment of restraint, renamed it One-Step Tropical Fruit Cake. As it turned out, Mrs. Schubert ended up winning $5,000 for her cake, which made everybody pretty mad, even the contestants who had been saying for days that they did not care who won, that winning meant nothing and was quite beside the point; the fact was that Sharon Schubert was a previous Bake-Off winner, having won $10,000 three years before for her Crescent Apple Snacks, and in addition had walked off with a trip to Puerto Vallarta in the course of this year's festivities. Most of the contestants felt she had won a little more than was really fair. But I'm getting ahead of the story.

The Pillsbury Company has been holding Bake-Offs since 1948, when Eleanor Roosevelt, for reasons that are not clear, came to give the first one her blessing. This year's took place from Saturday, February 24, through Tuesday, February 27, at the Beverly Hilton Hotel in Beverly Hills. One hundred contestants—97 of them women, 2 twelve-year-old boys, and 1 male graduate student—were winnowed down from a field of almost 100,000 entrants to compete for prizes in five categories: flour, frosting mix, crescent main dish, crescent dessert, and hot-roll mix. They were all brought, or flown, to Los Angeles for the Bake-Off itself, which took place on Monday, and a round of activities that included a tour of Universal Studios, a mini-version of television's *Let's Make A Deal* with Monty Hall himself, and a trip to Disneyland. The event is also attended by some 100 food editors, who turn it from a mere contest into the incredible publicity stunt Pillsbury intends it to be, and spend much of their time talking to each other about sixty-five new ways to use tuna fish and listening to various speakers lecture on the consumer movement and food and the appliance business. General Electric is co-sponsor of the event and donates a stove to each finalist, as well as the stoves for the Bake-Off; this year, it promoted a little Bake-Off of its own for the microwave oven, an appliance we were repeatedly told was the biggest improvement in cooking since the invention of the Willoughby System. Every one of the food editors seemed to know what the Willoughby System was, just as everyone seemed to know what Bundt pans were. "You will all be happy to hear," we were told at one point, "that only one of the finalists this year used a Bundt pan." The food editors burst into laughter at that point; I am not sure why. One Miss Alex Allard of San Antonio, Texas, had already won the microwave contest and $5,000, and she spent most of the Bake-Off turning out one Honey Drizzle Cake after another in the microwave ovens that ringed the Grand Ballroom of the Beverly Hilton Hotel. I never did taste the Honey Drizzle Cake, largely because I suspected—and this was weeks before the *Consumers Union* article on the subject—that microwave ovens were dangerous and probably caused peculiar diseases. If God had wanted us to make bacon in four minutes, He would have made bacon that cooked in four minutes.

"The Bake-Off is America," a General Electric executive announced just minutes before it began. "It's family. It's real people doing real things." Yes. The Pillsbury Bake-Off is an America that exists less and less, but exists nonetheless. It is women who still live on farms, who have six and seven children, who enter county fairs and sponsor 4-H Clubs. It is Grace Ferguson of Palm Springs, Florida, who entered the Bake-Off seventeen years in a row before reaching the finals this year, and who cooks at night and prays at the same time. It is Carol Hamilton, who once won a trip on a Greyhound bus to Hollywood for being the most popular girl in Youngstown, Ohio. There was a lot of talk at the Bake-Off about how the Bake-It-Easy theme had attracted a new breed of contestants this year, younger contestants—housewives, yes, but housewives who used whole-wheat flour and Granola and sour cream and similar supposedly hip ingredients in their recipes and were therefore somewhat more sophisticated, or urban, or something-of-the-sort than your usual Bake-Off contestant. There were a few of these—two, to be exact: Barbara Goldstein of New York City and Bonnie Brooks of Salisbury, Maryland, who actually visited the Los Angeles County Art Museum during a free afternoon. But there was also Suzie Sisson of Palatine, Illinois, twenty-five years old and the only Bundt-pan person in the finals, and her sentiments about life were the same as those that Bake-Off finalists presumably have had for years. "These are the beautiful people," she said, looking around the ballroom as she waited for her Bundt cake to come out of the oven. "They're not the little tiny rich people. They're nice and happy and religious types and family-oriented. Everyone talks about women's lib, which is ridiculous. If you're nice to your husband, he'll be nice to you. Your family is your job. They come first."

I was seven years old when the Pillsbury Bake-Off began, and as I grew up reading the advertisements for it in the women's magazines that were lying around the house, it always seemed to me that going to a Bake-Off would be the closest thing to a childhood fantasy of mine, which was to be locked overnight in a bakery. In reality, going to a Bake-Off *is* like being locked overnight in a bakery—a very bad bakery. I almost became sick right there on Range 95 after my sixth carbohydrate-packed sample—which happened, by coincidence, to be a taste of the aforementioned Mrs. Frisbie's aforementioned Sweet 'N Creamy Crescent Crisps.

But what is interesting about the Bake-Off—what is even significant about the event—is that it is, for the American housewife, what the Miss America contest used to represent to teen-agers. The pinnacle of a certain kind of achievement. The best in field. To win the Pillsbury Bake-Off, even to be merely a finalist in it, is to be a great housewife. And a creative housewife. "Cooking is very creative." I must have heard that line thirty times as I interviewed the finalists. I don't happen to think that cooking is very creative—what interests me about it is, on the contrary, its utter mindlessness and mathematical certainty. "Cooking is very relaxing"— that's my bromide. On the other hand, I have to admit that some of the recipes that were concocted for the Bake-Off, amazing combinations of frosting mix and marshmallows and peanut butter and brown sugar and chocolate, were practically awe-inspiring. And cooking, it is quite clear, is only a small part of the apparently frenzied creativity that flourishes in these women's homes. I spent quite a bit of time at the Bake-Off chatting with Laura Aspis of Shaker Heights, Ohio, a seven-time Bake-Off finalist and duplicate-bridge player, and after we had discussed her high-protein macaroons made with coconut-almond frosting mix and Granola, I noticed that Mrs. Aspis was wearing green nail polish. On the theory that no one who wears green nail polish wants it to go unremarked upon, I remarked upon it.

"That's not green nail polish," Mrs. Aspis said. "It's platinum nail polish that I mix with green food coloring."

"Oh," I said.

"And the thing of it is," she went on, "when it chips, it doesn't matter."

"Why is that?" I asked.

"Because it stains your nails permanently," Mrs. Aspis said.

"You mean your nails are permanently green?"

"Well, not exactly," said Mrs. Aspis. "You see, last week they were blue, and the week before I made purple, so now my nails are a combination of all three. It looks like I'm in the last throes of something."

On Sunday afternoon, most of the finalists chose to spend their free time sitting around the hotel and socializing. Two of them—Marjorie Johnson of Robbinsdale, Minnesota, and Mary Finnegan of Minneota, Minnesota—were seated at a little round table just off the Hilton ballroom talking about a number of things, including Tupperware. Both of them love Tupperware.

"When I built my new house," Mrs. Johnson said, "I had so much Tupperware I had to build a cupboard just for it." Mrs. Johnson is a very tiny, fortyish mother of three, and she and her dentist husband have just moved into a fifteen-room house she cannot seem to stop talking about. "We have this first-floor kitchen, harvest gold and blue, and it's almost finished. Now I have a second kitchen on my walk-out level and that's going to be harvest gold and blue, too. Do you know about the new wax Congoleum? I think that's what I put in—either that or Shinyl Vinyl. I haven't had to wash my floors in three months. The house isn't done yet because of the Bake-Off. My husband says if I'd spent as much time on it as I did on the Bake-Off, we'd be finished. I sent in sixteen recipes—it took me nearly a year to do it."

"That's nothing," said Mrs. Finnegan. "It took me twenty years before I cracked it. I'm a contest nut. I'm a thirty-times winner in the *Better Homes & Gardens* contest. I won a thousand dollars from Fleischmann's Yeast. I won Jell-O this year, I'm getting a hundred and twenty-five dollars' worth of Revere cookware for that. The Knox Gelatine contest. I've won seven blenders and a quintisserie. It does four things—fries, bakes, roasts, there's a griddle. I sold the darn thing before I even used it."

"Don't tell me," said Mrs. Johnson. "Did you enter the Crystal Sugar Name the Lake Home contest?"

"Did I enter?" said Mrs. Finnegan. "Wait till you see this."

She took a pen and wrote her submission on a napkin and held it up for Mrs. Johnson. The napkin read "Our Entry Hall." "I should have won that one," said Mrs. Finnegan. "I did win the Crystal Sugar Name the Dessert contest. I called it 'Signtation Squares.' I think I got a blender on that one."

"Okay," said Mrs. Johnson. "They've got a contest now, Crystal Sugar Name a Sauce. It has pineapple in it."

"I don't think I won that," said Mrs. Finnegan, "but I'll show you what I sent in." She held up the napkin and this time what she had written made sense. "Hawaiian More Chant," it said.

"Oh, you're clever," said Mrs. Johnson.

"They have three more contests so I haven't given up," said Mrs. Finnegan.

On Monday morning at exactly 9 a.m., the one hundred finalists marched four abreast into the Hilton ballroom, led by Philip Pillsbury, former chairman of the board of the company. The band played "Nothin' Says Lovin' Like Somethin' from the Oven," and when it finished, Pillsbury announced: "Now you one hundred winners can go to your ranges."

Chaos. Shrieking. Frenzy. Furious activity. Cracking eggs. Chopping onions. Melting butter. Mixing, beating, blending. The band perking along with such carefully selected tunes as "If I Knew You Were Coming I'd Have Baked a Cake." Contestants running to the refrigerators for more supplies. Floor assistants rushing dirty dishes off to unseen dishwashers. All two hundred members of the working press, plus television's Bob Barker, interviewing any finalist they could get to drop a spoon. At 9:34 a.m., Mrs. Lorraine Walmann submitted her Cheesy Crescent Twist-Ups to the judges and became the first finalist to finish. At 10 a.m., all the stoves were on, the television lights were blasting, the temperature in the ballroom was up to the mid-nineties, and Mrs. Marjorie Johnson, in the course of giving an interview about her house to the Minneapolis *Star*, had forgotten whether she had put one cup of sugar or two into her Crispy Apple Bake. "You know, we're building this new house," she was saying. "When I go back, I have to buy living-room furniture." By 11 a.m., Mae Wilkinson had burned her skillet corn bread and was at work on a second. Laura Aspis had lost her potholder. Barbara Bellhorn was distraught because she was not used to California apples. Alex Allard was turning out yet another Honey Drizzle Cake. Dough and flour were all over the floor. Mary Finnegan was fussing because the crumbs on her Lemon Cream Bars were too coarse. Marjorie Johnson was in the midst of yet another interview on her house. "Well, let me tell you," she was saying, "the shelves in the kitchen are built low...." One by one, the contestants, who were each given seven hours and four tries to produce two perfect samples of their recipes, began to finish up and deliver one tray to the judges and one tray to the photographer. There were samples everywhere, try this, try that, but after six tries, climaxed by Mrs. Frisbie's creation, I stopped sampling. The overkill was unbearable: none of the recipes seemed to contain one cup of sugar when two would do, or a delicate cheese when Kraft American would do, or an actual minced onion when instant minced onions would do. It was snack time. It was convenience-food time. It was less-work-for-Mother time. All I could think about was a steak.

By 3 p.m., there were only two contestants left—Mrs. Johnson, whose dessert took only five minutes to make but whose interviews took considerably longer, and Bonnie Brooks, whose third sour-cream-and-banana cake was still in the oven. Mrs. Brooks brought her cake in last, at 3:27 p.m., and as she did, the packing began. The skillets went into brown cartons, the measuring spoons into barrels, the stoves were dismantled. The Bake-Off itself was over—and all that remained was the trip to Disneyland, and the breakfast at the Brown Derby ... and the prizes.

And so it is Tuesday morning, and the judges have reached a decision, and any second now, Bob Barker is going to announce the five winners over national television. All the contestants are wearing their best dresses and smiling, trying to smile anyway, good sports all, and now Bob Barker is announcing the winners. Bonnie Brooks and her cake and Albina Flieller and her Quick Pecan Pie win $25,000 each. Sharon Schubert and two others win $5,000. And suddenly the show is over and it is time to go home, and the ninety-five people who did not win the twenty-fourth annual Pillsbury Bake-Off are plucking the orchids from the center-pieces, signing each other's programs, and grumbling. They are grumbling about Sharon Schubert. And for a moment, as I hear the grumbling everywhere—"It really isn't fair" ... "After all, she won the trip to Mexico"—I think that perhaps I am wrong about these women: perhaps they are capable of anger after all, or jealousy, or competitiveness, or something I think of as a human trait I can relate to. But the grumbling stops after a few minutes, and I find myself listening to Marjorie Johnson. "I'm so glad I didn't win the grand prize," she is saying, "because if you win that, you don't get to come back to the next Bake-Off. I'm gonna start now on my recipes for next year. I'm gonna think of something really good." She stopped for a moment. "You know," she said, "it's going to be very difficult to get back to normal living."

July, 1973

CRAZY LADIES

WASHINGTON is a city of important men and the women they married before they grew up. Is that how the saying goes? Something like that, anyway. All those tidy little summations of local phenomena—California is fine if you're an orange; first prize one week in Philadelphia, second prize two weeks in Philadelphia—turn out, after close inspection, to be even more accurate than they seemed at first hearing. But the one I wanted to talk about is the one about Washington.

I don't know a great deal about life in Washington for women—I spent a summer there once working in the White House, and my main memories of the experience have to do with a very bad permanent wave I have always been convinced kept me from having a meaningful relationship with President Kennedy—but that doesn't stop me from making generalizations about the place. Because it has always seemed obvious that life for women in Washington combined the worst qualities of the South and small-town life. Washington is a city of locker-room boys, and all the old, outmoded notions apply: men and women are ushered to separate rooms after dinner, sex is dirty, and they are still serving onion-soup dip. A married woman with any brains and personality at all is faced with a Hobson's choice: she can be her husband's appendage, and pay that price—and we have Joan Kennedy as the classic example of a woman who has. Or she can be a crazy lady.

I should clarify what I mean by crazy lady. In my youth—which ended about eight years ago—I occasionally had a date with someone who was very straight. Which is to say, square. In most relationships, I tend to be the straight one, cautious, conservative, not crossing on the Don't Walk, but whenever I was confronted with someone even squarer than I was, whenever I was confronted with a relationship where the role of the crazy person was up for grabs, I would leap in, say outrageous things, end the evening lying down in Times Square with a lampshade on my head. I wasn't a patch on Zelda Fitzgerald—I would never have leaped into the Plaza fountain for fear of ruining my hair—but I was in there doing my damnedest.

The crazy lady I have been thinking about apropos of all this is Barbara Howar. Mrs. Howar is not really crazy in any context where real craziness exists—in New York, she would just be another outspoken, somewhat bitchy woman. But Washington is a city that is an all-purpose straight man: you don't have to be a terribly funny joke to get laughs in Washington, and you don't have to be a terribly crazy person to seem about as loony as they come. Just jump into the Supreme Court fountain. Or refuse to go off with the ladies after dinner. Or have an affair. That's about all it takes.

Barbara Howar, who has written a book about her experiences in Washington, *Laughing All the Way* (Stein & Day), was a socialite who hooked up with Lynda Bird and Luci Baines in some inexplicable way having to do with wedding trousseaus and became a social light in the Johnson Administration. In an era not noted for its sophisticates, she became notorious for her sharp-tongued remarks, some of which were occasionally mistaken for wit and some of which were actually witty. Then she was dumped shortly before Luci's wedding, in a tacky and hilarious episode which confronted her with a true moral dilemma: should she warp her six-year-old daughter for life by withdrawing her from the role of flower girl in the ceremony, or warp her for life by letting her go on with it? After resolving this dilemma (she let her go on with it) and living through a decent period of social ostracism, Mrs. Howar emerged once again to resume her role as the town's Peck's Bad Girl.

As she recalls in her memoir, "I was filled with an uncontrollable desire to shock—to say or do anything that would raise voices and eyebrows or boredom's threshold. I had a natural ability to alienate people I found dull. I would rudely cut short any matron lady who dwelled too long on her wonderful children, her indispensable housekeeper, or her husband's unheralded political abilities. I once interrupted a woman deep into her monologue about the great Lone Star State with, 'If I hear one more exaggeration about Texas, I'm going to throw up on the Alamo.' I became incautious in my description of Texas habits, asking one gentleman sporting a hammered-silver belt studded with ersatz stones: 'Did you make it at summer camp?' And to a Dallas lady in reference to the Tex-Mex delicacy she had proudly served for dinner: 'Did you get this recipe off the back of a Fritos bag?'"

I liked *Laughing All the Way*—it happens to be far more charming than what I just quoted would indicate; it also happens to be fun to read. But I was surprised to find it as fascinating as I did, because what Barbara Howar has written, and I don't think it was unintentional, is almost a case study of a kind of woman and a kind of misdirected energy. And while I'm not sure any lesson or moral can be drawn from it—or if it can, I'm not about to do it—her floundering attempts to make a life and identity for herself are genuinely, and surprisingly, moving.

Barbara Howar came to Washington just out of finishing school and the South and went to work on Capitol Hill. She was pretty and blond and energetic and, as we used to say in high school, popular. As she writes, "I never wearied of flying on private planes to the Kentucky Derby with groups that included Aly Khan, of first nights of Broadway musicals. . . . But the tedium of clerical work dulled the excitement of my social life. I started doing bizarre things—my personal indicator of unrest—painting mailboxes shocking pink, leaping fully clothed into the Supreme Court fountain. One day I woke up disposed to do the only thing I had not yet tried: marriage." She married very well: her husband was a builder, heir to an Arab fortune, and she entered into the life of being his wife, working at charities, being photographed at luncheons, having parties and a family. Then 1964 came along, and because it was the thing to do that year, she went to work for the campaign of President Johnson.

It is altogether possible that had Barbara Howar married someone she was more capable of being an appendage of, none of what followed would have happened. Or it would have happened much later. In any event, she went off as Lady Bird Johnson's hairdresser on the campaign swing of the South, met a Johnson aide with whom she had an affair, and charmed the President to the point that he was soon holding her hand (and falling asleep) during White House movie screenings and whirling her about the dance floor at State functions. "I was *that* woman dancing with *the* President...," Mrs. Howar recalls. "It never occurred to me that I could distinguish myself in a more admirable fashion." *Woman's Wear Daily* began to follow her everywhere, *Life* magazine profiled her, and Maxine Cheshire watched as she danced on a tabletop in a white dress with gold chains she said "cut into my tender young flesh...just a little number the Marquis de Sade whipped up for me....

"There simply was no shutting me up. I had to tell every newspaper and magazine that Mrs. Johnson, a lady who spent every waking minute planting trees in ghettos and sprinkling tulip bulbs around settlement houses that had no plumbing, was 'off base' with her Beautification Program, that it was 'like buying a wig when your teeth are rotting.' I had to say in print that Mrs. Johnson's rich New York friends 'would be better advised to donate their money to countless endeavors like fighting street crime, and that to celebrate their philanthropy I would gladly wear a bronze plaque saying: TODAY I WAS NOT RAPED OR MUGGED THROUGH THE KIND GENEROSITY OF THE LASKER/LOEB FOUNDATIONS.'"

The affair with the Johnson aide continued and became a full-fledged Washington scandal; she left her husband and went off with her lover for a week in Jamaica. "In the sultry, alien surroundings of the Caribbean," she writes, in one of the more melodramatic sections of the book, "harsh reality became larger than my fantasy of finding peace by changing marriages. I became morbidly depressed for the first time in my life. I missed the children, my home, everything familiar and comfortable. I was melancholy and homesick, maudlin in my confusion, I wanted something to make me happy, something to give me reason not to care that half my life was over and that I had no real zest for finishing out the rest. Guilty and restless as before, I saw the future now as even more menacing. I wanted it all and I wanted out. It was the woman's primal feeling of being trapped, unable to live without marriage because it was all I knew, but incapable of projecting myself happily into more of the same. My anxieties grew. I had doubts about who I was and what I wanted to be. Why was I even in Jamaica?" At about this moment, Mrs. Howar's reveries were interrupted by a group of detectives, who burst in on her and the Johnson aide, ripped the strap on her nightgown, and took pictures. Mrs. Howar returned to Washington, reconciled for a time with her husband, and was promptly dropped by the Johnsons.

At this point, Barbara Howar's story became a morality tale. Her son gets spinal meningitis and almost dies. She finally leaves her husband. She develops a social conscience through a relationship with Bobby Darin, the singer, and becomes a star on a local television news show, where her standard operating procedure was to fling her newly acquired set of facts on life in the slums at her guests. "It was a long while," she writes, "before I learned that if there was anything worse than a bigoted keeper of the status quo, it was a recycled socialite with a newly aroused public conscience." Mrs. Howar complains, in what are straight women's movement terms, that her remarks on the air were not taken seriously because she was a woman. "If my male counterparts made strong critical statements, they were 'blunt' or 'forceful,' similar candor from television women is 'cutting,' 'catty,' and 'bitchy.'" She is right about the problems—though probably not in her own case. A typical moment in Mrs. Howar's television career was this remark, made as a criticism of the space program's all-white personnel: "If N.A.S.A. can train a monkey to operate the controls of a rocket, they can train a black man."

Laughing All the Way ends with a description of Mrs. Howar's disastrous and final experience in television, co-hosting a show with Mrs. David Susskind, and a marvelous chapter on her mother's death. "I am enormously saddened to understand that I would not be on my way to real peace if my mother were still alive," she writes. I don't know whether she is on her way to real peace—I would like to have heard a little more about that—but she *has* written a pretty good book about Barbara Howar. Which is more than I can say about her friend Willie Morris, who has also written a book about Barbara Howar this year, a novel called *The Last of the Southern Girls*. There is a point to be made here about borrowing material, and there is another point to be made about fact and fiction and the difference between them, but I don't want to get into that. I do want to say that I read Morris's book when I was almost finished with this column, and I note that we make some of the same points about Washington and women. I also note that he has the quote right. Washington is a city of men and the women they married when they were young. That's how it goes.

August, 1973

DOROTHY PARKER

ELEVEN years ago, shortly after I came to New York, I met a young man named Victor Navasky. Victor was trying relentlessly at that point to start a small humor magazine called *Monocle*, and there were a lot of meetings. Some of them were business meetings, I suppose; I don't remember them. The ones I do remember were pure social occasions, and most of them took place at the Algonquin Hotel. Every Tuesday at 6 p.m., we would meet for drinks there and sit around pretending to be the Algonquin Round Table. I had it all worked out: Victor got to be Harold Ross, Bud Trillin and C. D. B. Bryan alternated at Benchley, whoever was fattest and grumpiest got to be Alexander Woollcott. I, of course, got to be Dorothy Parker. It was all very heady, and very silly, and very self-conscious. It was also very boring, which disturbed me. Then Dorothy Parker, who was living in Los Angeles, gave a seventieth-birthday interview to the Associated Press, an interview I have always thought of as the beginning of the Revisionist School of Thinking on the Algonquin Round Table, and she said that it, too, had been boring. Which made me feel a whole lot better.

I had never really known Dorothy Parker at all. My parents, who were screenwriters, knew her when I was a child in Hollywood, and they tell me I met her at several parties where I was trotted out in pajamas to meet the guests. I don't remember that, and neither, I suspect, did Dorothy Parker. I met her again briefly when I was twenty. She was paying a call on Oscar Levant, whose daughter I grew up with. She was frail and tiny and twinkly, and she shook my hand and told me that when I was a child I had had masses of curly black hair. As it happens, it was my sister Hallie who had had masses of curly black hair. So there you are.

None of which is really the point. The point is the legend. I grew up on it and coveted it desperately. All I wanted in this world was to come to New York and be Dorothy Parker. The funny lady. The only lady at the table. The woman who made her living by her wit. Who wrote for *The New Yorker*. Who always got off the perfect line at the perfect moment, who never went home and lay awake wondering what she ought to have said because she had said exactly what she ought to have. I was raised on Dorothy Parker lines. Some were unbearably mean, and some were sad, but I managed to fuzz those over and remember the ones I loved. My mother had a first-rate Parker story I carried around for years. One night, it seems, Dorothy Parker was playing anagrams at our home with a writer named Sam Lauren. Lauren had just made the word "currie," and Dorothy Parker insisted there was no such spelling. A great deal of scrapping ensued. Finally, my mother said she had some curry in the kitchen and went to get it. She returned with a jar of Crosse & Blackwell currie and showed it to Dorothy Parker. "What do they know?" said Parker. "Look at the way they spell Crosse."

I have spent a great deal of my life discovering that my ambitions and fantasies—which I once thought of as totally unique—turn out to be clichés, so it was not a surprise to me to find that there were other young women writers who came to New York with as bad a Dorothy Parker problem as I had. I wonder, though, whether any of that still goes on. Whatever illusions I managed to maintain about the Parker myth were given a good sharp smack several years ago, when John Keats published a biography of her called *You Might As Well Live* (Simon & Schuster). By that time, I had come to grips with the fact that I was not, nor would I ever be, Dorothy Parker; but I had managed to keep myself from what anyone who has read a line about or by her should have known, which was simply that Dorothy Parker had not been terribly good at being Dorothy Parker either. In Keats's book, even the wonderful lines, the salty remarks, the softly murmured throwaways seem like dreadful little episodes in Leonard Lyons's column. There were the stories of the suicide attempts, squalid hotel rooms, long incoherent drunks, unhappy love affairs, marriage to a homosexual. All the early, sharp self-awareness turned to chilling self-hate. "Boy, did I think I was smart," she said once. "I was just a little Jewish girl trying to be cute."

A year or so after the Keats book, I read Lillian Hellman's marvelous memoir, *An Unfinished Woman* (Little, Brown). In it is a far more affectionate and moving portrait of Parker, one that manages to convey how special it was to be with her when she was at her best. "The wit," writes Hellman, "was never as attractive as the comment, often startling, always sudden, as if a curtain had opened and you had a brief and brilliant glance into what you would never have found for yourself." Still, the Hellman portrait is of a sad lady who misspent her life and her talent.

In one of several unbelievably stupid remarks that do so much to make the Keats biography as unsatisfying as it is, he calls Parker a "tiny, big-eyed feminine woman with the mind of a man." There are only a few things that remain clear to me about Dorothy Parker, and one of them is that the last thing she had was the mind of a man. *The Portable Dorothy Parker* (Viking) contains most of her writing; there are first-rate stories in it—"Big Blonde," of course—and first-rate light verse. But the worst work in it is characterized by an almost unbearably girlish sensibility. The masochist. The victim. The sentimental woman whose moods are totally ruled by the whims of men. This last verse, for example, from "To a Much Too Unfortunate Lady":

> He will leave you white with woe
> If you go the way you go.
> If your dreams were thread to weave,
> He will pluck them from his sleeve.
> If your heart had come to rest,
> He will flick it from his breast.
> Tender though the love he bore,
> You had loved a little more....
> Lady, go and curse your star,
> Thus Love is, and thus you are.

What seems all wrong about these lines now is not their emotion—the emotion, sad to say, is dead on—but that they seem so embarrassing. Many of the women poets writing today about love and men write with as much wit as Parker, but with a great deal of healthy anger besides. Like Edna St. Vincent Millay's poetry, which Parker was often accused of imitating, Dorothy Parker's poetry seems dated not so much because it is or isn't but because politics have made the sentiments so unfashionable in literature. The last thing I mean to write here is one of those articles about the woman artist as some sort of victim of a sexist society; it is, however, in Parker's case an easy argument to make.

And so there is the legend, and there is not much of it left. One no longer wants to be the only woman at the table. One does not want to spend nights with a group of people who believe that the smartly chosen rejoinder is what anything is about. One does not even want to be published in *The New Yorker*. But before one looked too hard at it, it was a lovely myth, and I have trouble giving it up. Most of all, I'm sorry it wasn't true. As Dorothy Parker once said, in a line she suggested for her gravestone: "If you can read this, you've come too close."

October, 1973

THE
LITTLEST
NIXON

SHE comes down the aisle, and the clothes are just right, Kimberly-knitted to the knee, and she walks in step with the government official, who happens to be H.E.W. Secretary Caspar Weinberger, and her face is perfect, not smiling, mind you—this is too serious an event for that—but bright, intent, as if she is absolutely fascinated by what he is saying. Perhaps she actually is. They take their places on the platform of the Right to Read Conference at Washington's Shoreham Hotel, and he speaks and she speaks and the director of Right to Read speaks. Throughout she listens raptly, smiles on cue, laughs a split second after the audience laughs. Perhaps she is actually amused. On the way out, she says she hopes she will be able to obtain a copy of the speech she has just sat through. Perhaps she actually thought it was interesting. There is no way to know. No way to break through. She has it all down perfectly. She was raised for this, raised to cut ribbons, and now that it has all gone sour, it turns out that she has been raised to deal with that, too.

The Washington press corps thinks that Julie Nixon Eisenhower is the only member of the Nixon Administration who has any credibility—and as one journalist put it, this is not to say that anyone believes what she is saying but simply that people believe *she* believes what she is saying. They will tell you that she is approachable, which is true, and that she is open, which is not. Primarily they find her moving. "There is something about a spirited and charming daughter speaking up for her father in his darkest hour that is irresistibly appealing to all but the most cynical." That from the *Daily News*. And this from NBC's Barbara Walters, signing off after Julie's last appearance on the *Today* show: "I think that no matter how people feel about your father, they're always very impressed to see a daughter defend her father that way."

There *is* something very moving about Julie Nixon Eisenhower—but it is not Julie Nixon Eisenhower. It is the *idea* of Julie Nixon Eisenhower, essence of daughter, a better daughter than any of us will ever be; it is almost as if she is the only woman in America over the age of twenty who still thinks her father is exactly what she thought he was when she was six. This idea is apparently so overwhelming in its appeal that some Washington reporters go so far as to say that Julie doesn't seem like a Nixon at all—a remark so patently absurd as to make one conclude either that they haven't heard a word she is saying or that they have been around Nixon so long they don't recognize a chocolate-covered spider when they see one.

I should point out before going any further that I have a special interest in Presidents' daughters, having spent a good thirty minutes in my youth wanting to be Margaret Truman. And even back then, I knew it was not a perfect existence— Secret Service men trailing you everywhere, life in a fishbowl, and so forth. Still, whatever the drawbacks, it seemed clear that if you were the President's daughter, you at least got to date a lot. The other attraction to the fantasy, I suppose, had to do with the fact that the role of the President's daughter is the closest thing there is in America to being a princess, the closest thing to having stature and privilege purely as a result of an accident of birth. It is one of life's little jokes that both America and Britain have suffered through remarkably similar princesses in recent years: the Johnson girls, the Nixon girls, and Princess Anne are all drab, dull young women who have managed to acquire enough poise and good grooming to get through the public events their parents do not have time to attend.

Julie and Tricia were born just as their father was beginning public life. They grew up in Washington as congressman's daughters, senator's daughters, and Vice-President's daughters. Then they moved to California to be gubernatorial candidate's daughters, and later to New York to be Presidential contender's daughters. After graduating from the Chapin School, Tricia went on to Finch College, Julie to Smith. There she began dating, and married—not a commoner, but a President's grandson. (David Eisenhower, with his endless tables of batting averages and illogical articles on the American left, is the perfect Nixon son-in-law. Still, he is not stupid. Last summer, after working as a sportswriter for the Philadelphia *Bulletin*, he was asked if he had any observations on the American press. "Yes," he reportedly said. "Journalists aren't nearly as interesting as they think they are.")

Marriage—which might logically have been expected to move Julie into a more removed and private existence—has instead strengthened and intensified her family connections and political role. During college, the Eisenhowers spent their summer vacations in a third-floor suite at the White House and took time off from school to campaign for Nixon's re-election. These days, they see Julie's parents several times a week; the Nixons often sneak off to eat with Julie and David in the $125,000 two-bedroom Bethesda home that Bebe Rebozo bought and rented to the Eisenhowers, presumably at well below its market price.

A few months ago, Julie took a full-time job at $10,000 a year at Curtis Publishing, where she is assistant editorial director of children's magazines and assistant editor of the *Saturday Evening Post*. She announced at the time that the children's magazine field attracted her because it would be impossible for her, as the President's daughter, to write for adult magazines on sensitive political subjects. An upcoming article for the *Saturday Evening Post*, however, while hardly on anything sensitive or political, is nonetheless on a topic that could not be more calculated to draw attention to her position: it is a profile of Alice Roosevelt Longworth, who is now eighty-nine and in the seventy-third year of her career as a President's daughter.

Julie, of course, is nothing like Alice Roosevelt, or any of the other flibbertigibbet President's daughters in the history of this country. In the months since the Watergate hearings began, she has become her father's principal defender, his First Lady in practice if not in fact. "It was something I took on myself," she said. "I just thought I had a story to tell, that there were certain points I could make, and I was very eager to do it. The idea that my father has to hide behind anyone's skirts is of course ludicrous." In any case, Julie's skirts were the only ones available: Pat Nixon is uncomfortable in press and television interviews, and Tricia is in New York. (Washington rumor has it that her husband, Edward Cox, and the President do not get on.) "And that leaves me," said Julie.

It has left her to make two appearances on the *Today* show, a television hookup with the BBC, a guest shot on Jack Paar's show. She has survived Kandy Stroud of *Women's Wear Daily* and lunch with Helen Thomas of the U.P.I. and Fran Lewine of the A.P. Odd little personal details about the President have slipped out during these interviews—whether deliberately or not. She has said that her father sometimes doesn't feel like getting up in the morning, that he took the role of devil's advocate in a family discussion on whether he should resign, that he often sits alone at night upstairs in the White House playing the piano. During her last appearance with Barbara Walters, whose interviews with her have been dazzling, she even came up with a sinister-influence theory of her own to explain everything: "Sometimes I think we were born under an unlucky star."

Her performances are always calm and professional and poised, her revelations just titillating enough, and after all, she's only a girl—and the combination of these has tended to draw attention away from the substantive things she is saying and the way she is saying them. Julie Eisenhower has developed—or been coached in—three basic approaches to answering questions. The first is not to answer the question at all. During her BBC appearance, an American woman living in England phoned in to say, "I would like Mrs. Eisenhower to know that her father's actions have made our position abroad untenable...it would be better if he came forward and answered questions himself instead of putting you in his place." Julie replied, "I'd like to ask...how she thinks my father can answer more on Watergate without pointing the finger at people who have not been indicted." This answer—in addition to skirting the question and making Nixon look like a man whose sole thought is of the Constitution—utterly overlooks the fact that almost everyone connected with Watergate has been called to testify, a good many have been indicted, and some have even been convicted.

The second approach is to point to the bright side. Thus, when she is asked about Watergate, she talks instead of her father's successes with China, Russia, and the Middle East crisis. When she is asked about the number of Presidential appointees who have been forced to resign, she mentions Henry Kissinger and Ron Ziegler, whom she once called "a man of great integrity." "And I'd go beyond that," she said once. "I'd say that many of these people we're talking about, these aides, were great Americans, really devoted to their country, and they didn't make any money on Watergate, they didn't do anything for personal gain. They made mistakes, errors in judgment. I don't think they're evil men."

The third, and most classic, of Mrs. Eisenhower's techniques is simply to put the blame elsewhere—on the press. She combines the Middle American why-doesn't-the-press-ever-print-good-news theme with good old-fashioned Nixon paranoia. I spoke with her the other day for five minutes, and she spent most of that time complaining that her mother had met the day before with a group from the Conference on the Role of Women in the Economy, and not one word about it had been printed in the papers. "Instead we get all these negative things," she said. When she was asked recently what she thought of Barry Goldwater's charge that her father's credibility was at an all-time low, she replied: "Barry Goldwater also had a press conference during this whole period . . . and he said that the press were hounds of destruction. I don't think he meant all of the press, but, um, Goldwater *is* a quotable man, isn't he? I didn't hear *that* on the networks. But when he says [my father's] credibility is at an all-time low, that *is* on the networks."

The only questions that stump Julie Eisenhower at all are the ones that concern her father's personality. She has said that she is sick of telling reporters what a warm, human person he is—a fact that fortunately has not stopped reporters from pressing her to give examples. One story she produced recently to show what a card her father can be in his off moments concerned the time her husband, David, took the wheel of Bebe Rebozo's yacht—and the President, in response, appeared on deck wearing not one but two life preservers. "He is quite a practical joker," she said on an-

other occasion. "He likes to tease and he likes to plan surprises when he can. Things like getting birthday candles for
a cake that don't blow out. You know, all nice and lit and
you sit there huffing and puffing and they don't go out. . . .
Things like that."

There is no point in dwelling too heavily on the implications of a daughter who has managed to play a larger role
in her father's life than his wife seems to. And there is also
no point in wondering what is going to happen to Julie
Eisenhower's view of her father if the fall actually comes. It
is safe to say that breeding will win out, and all the years of
growing up in that family will protect her from any insight
at all, will lead her to conclude that he was quite simply done
in by malicious, unpatriotic forces. What is clear, though, is
that Julie Nixon Eisenhower is fighting for herself and her
position as hard as she is fighting for her father and his. She
once said that if her father was forced out of office, she
would "just fold up and wither and fall away." What is more
likely is that she will deal with that, too, vanish for a couple
of years, and then crop up in politics again. That, after all,
is what Nixons do, and that, in the end, is all she is.

December, 1973

DIVORCE, MARYLAND STYLE

THE *Ladies' Home Journal* is after her. *Cosmopolitan* is after her. I am after her. All of us think that there is something to the story of Barbara Mandel, something positively paradigmatic. After all, what happened to Barbara Mandel last year happens to thousands of American women. After thirty-two years of marriage, her husband left her for another woman. Moved into a hotel. Called a lawyer. It happens every day. The difference, in this case, was that Barbara Mandel's husband was Marvin Mandel, the governor of the state of Maryland. And Barbara Mandel was having none of it.

It is safe to say that there was no way Marvin Mandel could have left his wife that would have made her happy; nonetheless, he managed to leave her in a way that was bound to humiliate her as completely as possible. To begin with, he did not even tell her himself. Well, that's not entirely fair: for two years he had been telling her he wanted a divorce, and for two years she had been telling him she would never give him one. But he never told her he was actually moving out; the morning he did, July 3, 1973, he arranged an appointment for her with the family doctor and had him break the news. His press secretary read her the statement over the telephone. And when Barbara Mandel called her husband to beg him to hold off, he informed her that it was too late; the press had already been given the statement.

"I would like to announce that I am separated from Mrs. Mandel," it read. "My decision and separation are final and irrevocable, and I will take immediate action to dissolve the marriage. . . . I am in love with another woman, Mrs. Jeanne Dorsey, and I intend to marry her. Mrs. Mandel and I have had numerous discussions about this matter and she is completely aware of my feelings, of my actions, and of my intentions. . . . Mrs. Mandel and I no longer share mutual interests nor are our lives mutually fulfilling. . . ."

There was not a mention of the good years, the old times spent growing up as childhood sweethearts in northwest Baltimore. There was not a mention of what she had done for him, all those hands she shook, all those ward heelers' names she memorized, all those rooms in the governor's mansion she repainted. He was leaving her. He was leaving her publicly. He was stripping her of her only weapon—the threat of exposing his liaison—by announcing it himself. Barbara Mandel, First Lady of Maryland—that was how she signed the souvenir ashtrays and the 8″ × 10″ glossies—reacted by refusing to go.

"The governor crawled out of my bed this morning," she told the reporters she telephoned that afternoon. "He has never slept anyplace but with me. I think the strain of the job has gotten to him. I'm surprised. Marvin has not discussed this with me. I don't know what in the world he's talking about. I hope the governor will come to his senses on this. You don't take thirty-two years of married life and throw them down the drain." Mrs. Mandel added that she thought her husband "should see a psychiatrist." In the meantime, she said, she would wait for him in the mansion.

So far, a fairly ordinary American tragedy. A woman invests her life in her husband's career, and he pays her back by leaving her. A woman grows up in a society where the only option seems to be to dedicate herself to her husband. "My case is just different because I helped to make him governor," Mrs. Mandel said.

But, of course, that was a big difference—and that is where the case departs abruptly from the paradigm. Barbara Mandel responded to her husband's rejection not just as a wounded wife but as a seasoned politician. She carefully leaked tidbits of information to selected reporters. She allowed one reporter to negotiate on her behalf with the governor's chief aide. Her statement on July 3—which seems on the surface quite hysterical—carefully left the governor a face-saving way to return: he could simply admit that she was right, the pressures of the job *had* gotten to him; now he had come to his senses. Hell hath no fury, it is true; at the same time, it was clear that part of Mrs. Mandel's fury came not just from the fact that there was another woman involved, but also from the suspicion that the other woman wanted to use her husband and his position exactly as much as Mrs. Mandel did.

Marvin Mandel was a young Baltimore lawyer in 1952 when he first entered the state legislature. He was diligent and hard-working; in addition, he was thoroughly introverted. His outgoing wife—who was known as Bootsie, a nickname that she inexplicably rhymes with "footsie"—campaigned and went everywhere with him; she provided the warmth and earthiness he was chronically unable to convey. Mandel rose to become speaker of the House of Delegates. In 1969, after Spiro Agnew left the governorship to become Vice-President, the Mandels moved into the fifty-three-room Georgian governor's mansion in Annapolis. By this time, the governor's relationship with Mrs. Dorsey had been common knowledge around the State House for years; one of Mrs. Dorsey's four children recently told the Washington *Post* that his mother had been seeing Mandel since 1960. Mrs. Dorsey, now thirty-six, was divorced a few years ago from another Maryland legislator; she is a Democrat who served as police commissioner during a stint on her town board. ("I'm not a big story," she told the *Post*'s Judy Bachrach recently, "and there's no reason why I should open my private life to you. Now, frankly, there is a big story and it's right here in Leonardtown. We have this terrific sewage problem.")

Bootsie Mandel was never in the tradition of great first ladies—but compared with her predecessor, she did an energetic, creditable job, and she became more involved in it as her isolation from the governor increased. "God damn it, I'm nothing around here," she told one of her husband's supporters early in his first term. "Before he was governor, I used to drive him everywhere. Now he has a state trooper. I used to help him with his speeches. Now he has a speechwriter. What good am I?" What good she did had mainly to do with the mansion. She refurbished it, printed up lavish programs describing its interior, appeared at charity luncheons to announce that twice-a-week tours through it were available.

At the same time, she had a habit of getting everything she did slightly wrong. At one point, she discovered that a portrait hanging in the mansion had a label attributing it to Hogarth; she promptly insured it for $300,000, scheduled a ceremony and surprise announcement, and was informed by a prominent art historian that the painting wasn't a Hogarth at all. Several years ago, she confounded the entire state legislature by inviting the wives to the annual party celebrating the legislature's adjournment; the party had traditionally been an event for the politicians to be with whatever women they had been seeing on the sly during the session. Said one Baltimore assemblyman: "You cannot overestimate the panic that went through this place that day."

Governor Mandel's relationship with Mrs. Dorsey became increasingly open. In December, 1970, his unmarked state police car hit another car in Prince Georges County and the driver of the other car was killed. The governor refused to say what he was doing in an unmarked car after midnight; then he said he had been at a secret political meeting. Reporters checked and could not find any other politicians who had been to a meeting with the governor that night. When they asked whether he hadn't in fact been returning from St. Marys County, where Mrs. Dorsey lived, he declined comment. At about that time, Mrs. Mandel apparently found out that the situation was serious and began to pump her friends for information. Sometimes she asked straight out; more often, she attempted an approach she seemed to believe was devious. "What do you think the Jewish community would say about a governor who left his wife for another woman?" she asked the wife of one of her husband's associates.

Within a few weeks of the governor's walkout, Mrs. Mandel realized she had made a terrible mistake. She had counted on her friends to side with her—and they sided with the governor and his power. She had counted on major political repercussions—but there was only a brief flurry of mail support from middle-aged women. She had counted on seeming to be a force for morality—and instead she became an object of ridicule. "She was playing cards in a game that had ended," said one Maryland politician. "It had ended in American politics, in American life, even ended in her narrow circle. Divorce just doesn't mean that much anymore."

Bootsie carried on. She alerted the press as to her comings and goings. She appeared at a Washington literary party and identified herself as the woman who had knocked Elizabeth Taylor and Richard Burton's breakup off the front page. She spoke to a group of Democratic women, many of whom cried as she vowed to continue as first lady. "I want you to know that I am a very proud woman," she said, "very very proud of everything I've done since I've been a little girl. Life does not always work out the way you want it. . . ."

In the end, what kept Barbara Mandel in the governor's mansion as long as she stayed was not the pathetic hope that her husband would return—she had long given up on that—but the fact that her presence there was the only wedge she had to negotiate a substantial money settlement. Mandel's first offer to his wife, she told friends, was $6,250 a year, a quarter of his yearly salary as governor. Her lawyer ultimately negotiated a six-figure settlement. And on December 20, with a crowd of reporters standing outside the wrought-iron gates, Barbara Mandel moved out, with her hope chest, love seat, artificial flower centerpieces, and eight wardrobe boxes of clothing. "Five and a half months have passed and our marriage has not returned to normal," she said. "Therefore, with deep regret, I am leaving the mansion."

She moved to a two-bedroom apartment in Baltimore—in the same complex where her married son and daughter live—and when I reached her on the telephone, she told me she preferred not to say anything. "I'm very busy," she said. Doing what? I asked. "Just the normal things," she said, "the normal things you have to do for yourself."

"I'll tell you a story," one of her friends said a few days ago. "The day after Marvin moved out, last July, Bootsie went to the family cemetery. She sat looking at the graves, and she wished that he were dead. She felt she would have been better off as a widow. I can't help thinking she was right."

January, 1974

NO, BUT I READ THE BOOK

SUPPOSE it is completely presumptuous for me to write even one word on the saga of Pat and Bill and Lance and Kevin and Grant and Delilah and Michele Loud. Last year, I managed to miss every single episode of *An American Family*. But I did catch the Louds on the talk shows, and it seemed to me at the time that, with the possible exception of Tiny Tim, no group of people had ever passed so quickly from being celebrities to being freaks. I was amazed at the amount of time they lingered on, being analyzed in print, taking up space on the air, stealing valuable time from any number of people I would prefer to have read about or seen, even including Shecky Greene. Finally, though, like a toothache, the Louds went away. And the other day, when Pat Loud's book arrived in the mail, I felt terrible that I had not spent the months of their absence grateful for it; it is always easier to have a toothache return when you have at least had the sense to appreciate how wonderful it was not to have had one.

Pat Loud: A Woman's Story was written by Mrs. Loud with Nora Johnson, and the publicity director at Coward, McCann & Geoghegan assures me that its style—which is slick and show-biz rat-a-tat-tat—reflects Mrs. Loud's way of speaking exactly. "Gloria was a lamb chop." "Rose gardens he doesn't walk through." Like that. The book itself is sad and awful, and at times quite fascinating and moving. All these adjectives ring a bell: it seems to me that they were applied to the television series as well. In fact, the only thing about Pat Loud's book that is different from the television series that propelled her into her book contract is that no one who reads it will ever wonder Why She Did It. She did it because she wanted to tell her side. She did it because she had very little else to do. And she did it because she has come to believe that her brand of letting-it-all-hang-out candor is valuable to others in her position. Will she ever learn?

"Every other writer and cocktail circuit sociologist is contemplating the problem of the 46-year-old mother-housewife who suddenly isn't needed anymore," Mrs. Loud writes. "But most of these 'problem women' never had what has saved me, at least so far, from that devastating moment of truth: instant fame." The television show may not have saved Pat Loud from the truth—her own head seems to have done that job perfectly well. But the experience certainly confused her, and confused the issues involved to boot. Pat Loud's book is not the straight I-found-myself-through-divorce women's lib confessional; her case is too unusual. Rather, it is a rambling, perplexing, contradictory account by a woman who is trying, and failing, to make some sense out of a series of events that probably defy sensible explanation.

The real story of the Loud marriage, as told in this book, is a good deal more complicated and tacky, mainly tacky, than what I gather came out in the television series. The Louds and their five children lived in Santa Barbara, California, Pat working hard at being Supermom, Bill at his strip-mining-equipment business. As the marriage went on and the number of children increased, Mrs. Loud began finding telltale clues around the house. First a love letter to Bill from another woman, then a loose glove in his suitcase, lipstick on his handkerchiefs, a brochure from a Las Vegas hotel. The love letter enraged her so that she packed her four children into the family car—she was pregnant with the fifth—and drove off into the night. As it turned out, she did not get very far; Mrs. Loud, who has no selectivity index whatsoever, explains: "When I'm pregnant, I have the trots all the time, and sometimes it's really essential to get to a john fast . . . and there wasn't any gas station. . . . So finally I turned around and went home." In 1966, she found a set of her husband's cuff links, engraved "To Bill, Eternally Yours, Kitty," and all hell broke loose. Her husband assured her he had bought the cuff links in a pawn shop, but she did not believe him. So she snuck off, had an extra set of his office keys made, and while he was off on a business trip she went to look through his files.

"It was all there," she writes, "as though it had been waiting for me for years—credit card slips telling of restaurants I'd never been to and hotels I'd never stayed at, plane tickets to places I'd never seen, even pictures of Bill and his girls as they grinned and screwed their way around the countryside."

Bill Loud returned from his business trip. Pat Loud slugged him, in front of the children. He slugged her back, in front of the children. They both went to see a psychiatrist. They both stopped seeing the psychiatrist. They spent night after night getting drunk as Bill Loud recited the intimate sexual details of his infidelities. The subject of open marriage was introduced. Pat Loud began going to local bars during lunch and picking up businessmen. "We would have a few drinks and some tortillas," she recalls. "Then we would let nature take its course." She threatened divorce. He started seeing his women again. And in the midst of this idyllic existence, Craig Gilbert, a film-maker with a contract from public television, came into their home and told them he was looking for "an attractive, articulate California family" to do a one-hour special about.

It is impossible to read this book and not suspect that Craig Gilbert knew exactly what he was doing when he picked the Louds, knew after ten minutes with them and the clinking ice in their drinks that he had found the perfect family to show exactly what he must have intended to show all along— the emptiness of American family life. Occasionally, in the course of this book, Pat Loud starts to suspect this, nibbles around it, yaps like a puppy at the ankles of truth, then tosses the idea aside in favor of loftier philosophical pronouncements. "If he knew it," she concludes, "it was not necessarily because he actively smelled it about us, but because he knew in a way what we didn't—that life is lousy and it's tragic and it's supposed to be and you can pretend otherwise if you want, but if you do, you're wrong."

Gilbert had no trouble persuading the Louds to cooperate.

Bill had always been outgoing and exhibitionistic. Pat, for her part, saw the show as a way to appear as she had always wanted to—the perfect mother, cheerfully beating egg whites in her copper bowls. When Gilbert informed them that the show was going to be so good that he would shoot enough for five specials and then twelve, the Louds consented, apparently without a tremor of anxiety.

"Of course," Pat Loud writes, "if you're going to be in print or on the radio or TV, you can't help thinking of all the people who will read or see you, and the first ones I thought of were all Bill's women. There they would sit in frowzy little rented rooms scattered about California, Oregon, Washington, and Arizona, little gifts from Bill here and there, a memento from some trip or something he'd bought them, pathetic scraps of forgotten pleasure in their failed and lonely worlds. Their bleached blond hair would be falling sloppily out of its hairpins and their enormous breasts would be falling equally sloppily out of their torn, spotty negligees as they clutched their glasses of Scotch and rested their fat ankles on footstools to relieve their aching, varicose veins.... In pathetic, panting interest they would turn on their televisions to look at the Louds, and they would weep. ... If they'd had Bill for a few hours or days, if they'd had a few sessions of what they probably thought of as blinding ecstasy, I had had him a thousand times more."

Pat Loud offers a number of other explanations as to why her family agreed to Gilbert's proposal—the one she seems to believe most firmly is that anyone would have. But she is less sure about why the reaction to the show was so enormous. "What nerve have we touched?" she asks at one point. "I would like to know; I would really like to know." I suspect I know. I think the American public has an almost insatiable need to feel superior to people who appear to have everything, and the Louds were the perfect vehicle to fill that need. There they were, a beautiful family with a beautiful house with a beautiful pool, and one son was a homosexual, the rest of the children lolled about, uninterested in anything, and the marriage was breaking up. All of it was on television, in *cinéma vérité*—a medium that at its best (I'm thinking of the Maysleses' *Salesman* and the Canadian Film Board's *Lonely Boy* and *The Most*) has always tended to specialize in a certain amount of implicit condescension.

It is on the subject of the making of the series that Pat Loud is most interesting. *Cinéma vérité* film-makers have always insisted that after a time, their subjects forget the cameras are there, but as Pat Loud makes clear, it's just not possible. "You can't forget the camera," she writes, "and everybody's instinct is to try and look as good as possible for it, all the time, and to keep kind of snapping along being active, eager, cheery, and productive. Out go those moments when you're just in a kind of nothing period.... You don't realize how many of those you have until you're trying not to have them.... And what you also don't realize is that you *have* to have them—they're like REM sleep."

Ultimately, Pat Loud seems to have come to believe that she owed more to the film-makers than she did to herself or her husband; any concept of dignity or privacy she may have had evaporated in the face of pressure from them. Again she nibbles around the edges of this, almost but not quite getting it, but the suggestions of what happened are there: the illiterate Californians trying to impress the erudite Easterners; the boring, slothful family attempting to come up with a dramatic episode to justify all that footage; the woman who had always tried to please men—first her father, then her husband—now transferring it all to Craig Gilbert.

And when, in the course of events, Pat Loud decided she wanted a divorce, Craig Gilbert convinced her that she owed it to him, to all of them, to do it on the air. "If I decided to divorce during the filming," Mrs. Loud says Gilbert told her, "I must be honest enough to do it openly and not confuse the issue further by refusing to allow it to be shot." Again she almost has it, almost sees how she was conned, and then falls into utter nonsense. "Couldn't it be," she asks, "that since circumstance and fate had put me in a position to rip away the curtain of hypocrisy, that maybe, just maybe, we could help other families face their problems more honestly?" And then she switches gears, and makes sense again: "A psychiatrist told a friend of mine recently that in his experience he'd found that there is almost always a third force present when divorce finally happens. The miserable marriage can wobble on for years on end, until something or somebody comes along and pushes one of the people over the brink.... It's usually another man ... or another woman ... or possibly a supportive psychiatrist; in my case, it was a whole production staff and a camera crew...."

And so the marriage and the television series ended, and along came the notoriety. And now there is the book, and there will be more: more talk shows, more interviews. It all seems sad; there is no way to read this book and not feel that this bumbling woman is in way over her head. She has made a fool of herself on television, and now she is making a fool of herself in print. She does not understand that it is just as hard to be honest successfully as it is to lie successfully. And now, God help her, she has moved to New York. She will get a job, she tells us at the end of the book, and perhaps she will be able to fulfill her fantasy. Here is Pat Loud's last fantasy. She's at this swell New York cocktail party, "exchanging terribly New York in-type gossip about who's backing what new play and who got how much for the paperback rights to Philip Roth's latest," and there is this man who takes her to dinner, and then to bed, and they have a wonderful affair. "I'm not saying he would solve everything, or pick up the pieces, or even make me happy. Nor is he as important as a good job. But the nice thing about fantasies is that you don't have to explain them to anybody. They are absolutely free." There she goes again, almost making sense, talking about the importance of work, and the need not to look to anyone for the solution of her problems, and then she blows it all. "They are absolutely free." That's the thing about fantasies. They're not absolutely free. Sometimes you pay dearly for them. Which is something Pat Loud ought to have learned by now. Will she ever?

March, 1974

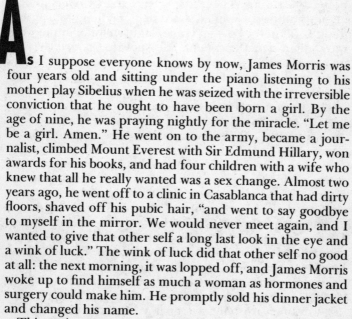

CONUNDRUM

As I suppose everyone knows by now, James Morris was four years old and sitting under the piano listening to his mother play Sibelius when he was seized with the irreversible conviction that he ought to have been born a girl. By the age of nine, he was praying nightly for the miracle. "Let me be a girl. Amen." He went on to the army, became a journalist, climbed Mount Everest with Sir Edmund Hillary, won awards for his books, and had four children with a wife who knew that all he really wanted was a sex change. Almost two years ago, he went off to a clinic in Casablanca that had dirty floors, shaved off his pubic hair, "and went to say goodbye to myself in the mirror. We would never meet again, and I wanted to give that other self a long last look in the eye and a wink of luck." The wink of luck did that other self no good at all: the next morning, it was lopped off, and James Morris woke up to find himself as much a woman as hormones and surgery could make him. He promptly sold his dinner jacket and changed his name.

This entire mess could doubtless have been avoided had James Morris been born an Orthodox Jew (in which case he could have adopted the standard Jewish prayer thanking God for *not* making him a woman) or had he gone to see a good Freudian analyst, who might have realized that any young boy sitting under a piano was probably looking up his mother's skirt. But no such luck. James Morris has become Jan Morris, an Englishwoman who wears sweater sets and pearls, blushes frequently, bursts into tears at the littlest things, and loves having a gossip with someone named Mrs. Weatherby. Mrs. Weatherby, Morris writes, "really is concerned...about my migraine yesterday; and when I examine myself I find that I am no less genuinely distressed to hear that Amanda missed the school outing because of her ankle."

Conundrum is Jan Morris's book about her experience, and I read it with a great deal of interest, largely because I always wanted to be a girl, too. I, too, felt that I was born into the wrong body, a body that refused, in spite of every imprecation and exercise I could manage, to become anything but the boyish, lean thing it was. I, too, grew up wishing for protectors, strangers to carry my bags, truck drivers to whistle out windows. I wanted more than anything to be something I will never be—feminine, and feminine in the worst way. Submissive. Dependent. Soft-spoken. Coquettish. I was no good at all at any of it, no good at being a girl; on the other hand, I am not half-bad at being a woman. In contrast, Jan Morris is perfectly awful at being a woman; what she has become instead is exactly what James Morris wanted to become those many years ago. A girl. And worse, a forty-seven-year-old girl. And worst of all, a forty-seven-year-old *Cosmopolitan* girl. To wit:

"So I well understand what Kipling had in mind, about sisters under the skin. Over coffee a lady from Montreal effuses about Bath—'I don't know if you've done any traveling yourself' (not too much, I demurely lie) 'but I do feel it's important, don't you, to see how other people really live.' I bump into Jane W_____ in the street, and she tells me about Archie's latest excess—'Honestly, Jan, you don't know how lucky you are.' I buy some typing paper—'How lovely to be able to write, you make me feel a proper dunce'—and walking home again to start work on a new chapter, find that workmen are in the flat, taking down a picture-rail. One of them has knocked my little red horse off the mantelpiece, chipping its enameled rump. I restrain my annoyance, summon a fairly frosty smile, and make them all cups of tea, but I am thinking to myself, as they sheepishly help themselves to sugar, a harsh feminist thought. It would be a man, I think. Well it would, wouldn't it?"

It is a truism of the women's movement that the exaggerated concepts of femininity and masculinity have done their fair share to make a great many people unhappy, but nowhere is this more evident than in Jan Morris's mawkish and embarrassing book. I first read of Morris in a Sunday *New York Times Magazine* article that brought dignity and real sensitivity to Morris's obsession. But Morris's own sensibility is so giddy and relentlessly cheerful that her book has almost no dignity at all. What she has done in it is to retrace his/ her life (I am going to go crazy from the pronouns and adjectives here) by applying sentimental gender judgments to everything. Oxford is wonderful because it is feminine. Venice is sublime because it is feminine. Statesmen are dreadful because they are masculine. "Even more than now," Morris writes of his years as a foreign correspondent, "the world of affairs was dominated by men. It was like stepping from cheap theater into reality, to pass from the ludicrous goings-on of minister's office or ambassador's study into the private house behind, where women were to be found doing real things, like bringing up children, painting pictures, or writing home."

And as for sex—but let Morris tell you about men and women and sex. "You are doubtless wondering, especially if you are male, what about sex? . . . One of the genuine and recurrent surprises of my life concerns the importance to men of physical sex. . . . For me the actual performance of the sexual act seemed of secondary importance and interest. I suspect this is true for most women. . . . In the ordinary course of events [the sex act] struck me as slightly distasteful, and I could imagine it only as part of some grand act, a declaration of absolute interdependence, or even a sacrifice."

Over the years, Morris saw a number of doctors, several of whom suggested he try homosexuality. (He had tried it several times before, but found it aesthetically unpleasant.) A meeting was arranged with the owner of a London art gallery. "We had a difficult lunch together," Morris writes, "and he made eyes at the wine waiter over the fruit salad." The remark is interesting, not just because of its hostility toward homosexuals but also because Jan Morris now makes exactly those same sorts of eyes at wine waiters—on page 150 of her book, in fact.

As James turns into a hermaphrodite and then into Jan, the prose in the book, which is cloying enough to begin with, turns into a kind of overembellished, simile-laden verbiage that makes the style of Victorian women novelists seem spare. Exclamation points and italicized words appear with increasing frequency. Everything blushes. James Morris blushes. His "small breasts blossomed like blushes." He starts talking to the flowers and wishing them a Happy Easter. He becomes even more devoted to animals. He is able for the first time ("the scales dropped from my eyes") to look out a plane window and see things on the ground below not as cars and homes seen at a distance but "Lo!...as dolls' houses and dinky toys." Shortly before the operation, he and his wife, Elizabeth, whose understanding defies understanding, take a trip, both as women, through Oregon. "How merrily we traveled!" Morris writes. "What fun the Oregonians gave us! How cheerfully we swapped badinage with boatmen and lumberjacks, flirtatious garage hands and hospitable trappers! I never felt so liberated, or more myself, nor was I ever more fond of Elizabeth. 'Come on in, girls,' the motel men would say, and childish though I expect it sounds to you, silly in itself, perhaps a little pathetic, possibly grotesque, still if they had touched me with an accolade of nobility, or clad me ceremonially in crimson, I could not have been more flattered." The only thing Morris neglects to write into this passage is a little face with a smile on it.

Morris is infuriatingly vague about the reactions of her children (she blandly insists they adjusted perfectly) and of Elizabeth (she says they are still the closest of friends). "I am not the first," Morris writes, "to discover that one recipe for an idyllic marriage is a blend of affection, physical potency and sexual incongruity." (Idyllic marriage? Where your husband becomes a lady? I suppose we owe this to creeping Harold-and-Vitaism; still, it is one of the more ridiculous trends of recent years to confuse great friendships with great marriages; great marriages are when you have it all.) As for her new sex life, Jan Morris lyrically trills that her sexuality is now unbounded. But how?

Unfortunately, she is a good deal more explicit about the details of what she refers to as "truly the symptoms of womanhood." "The more I was treated as a woman, the more woman I became," she writes. "I adapted willy-nilly. If I was assumed to be incompetent at reversing cars, or opening bottles, oddly, incompetent I found myself becoming. If a case was thought too heavy for me, inexplicably I found it so myself. . . . I discovered that even now men prefer women to be less informed, less able, less talkative, and certainly less self-centered than they are themselves; so I generally obliged them. . . . I did not particularly want to be good at reversing cars, and did not in the least mind being patronized by illiterate garage-men, if it meant they were going to give me some extra trading stamps. . . . And when the news agent seems to look at me with approval, or the man in the milk-cart smiles, I feel absurdly elated, as though I have been given a good review in the Sunday *Times*. I know it is non-sense, but I cannot help it."

The truth, of course, is that Jan Morris does not know it is nonsense. She thinks that is what it is about. And I wonder about all this, wonder how anyone in this day and age can think that this is what being a woman is about. And as I wonder, I find myself thinking a harsh feminist thought. It would be a man, I think. Well, it would, wouldn't it?

June, 1974

THE MINK COAT

THINK it was about 1954 when my mother got her mink. A Beverly Hills furrier had run into some difficulty with the Internal Revenue Service and he was selling off his coats. My mother would never have bought anything wholesale— she disapproved of it on grounds that I never understood but later came to suspect had something to do with being the daughter of a garment salesman—but there was a distinction between buying wholesale and getting a good price. She got a good price. It was an enormous mink. A tent. It came to her ankles, and at least two people could have fitted under it. The skins were worked vertically. I did not know this at the time. I did not know much of anything at the time, much less anything about the way mink skins were worked. A few years later, when I knew, all the furriers in America decided to work the skins horizontally; when I heard about it, I instantly understood that it would not make her happy to be wearing an Old Mink. But she always pretended that things like that meant nothing to her. She was a career woman who was defiant about not being like the other mothers, the other mothers who played canasta all day and went to P.T.A. meetings and wore perfume and talked of hemlines; she hated to shop, hated buying clothes. Once a year, after my father had nagged her into it, she would go off to a fashionable ladies' clothing store on Wilshire Boulevard and submit to having a year's supply of clothing brought to her in a dressing room larger than my current apartment. She grumbled throughout. I thought she was mad. Now I understand.

My guess is that my father paid for the mink, wrote the check for it—but he did not *buy* it for her. My parents worked together, wrote together, and there was no separation between his money and hers. That was important. Beverly Hills was a place where the other mothers wore minks their husbands had bought them. They would come to dinner. The maid would bring the coats upstairs and lay them on my mother's bed. Dozens of them, silver, brown, black, all of them lined with what seemed like satin and monogrammed by hand with initials, three initials. I would creep into the bedroom and lie on the bed and roll over them and smell the odd and indescribable smell of the fur. Other children grow up loving the smell of fresh-cut grass and raked leaves; I grew up in Beverly Hills loving the smell of mink, the smell of the pavement after it rained, and the smell of dollar bills. A few years ago, I went back to Beverly Hills and all I could smell was jasmine, and I realized that that smell had always been there and I had never known it.

My mother wore the mink for years. She wore it through the horizontal period and into another vertical period, but it never became fashionable again; by the time vertical skins were back, furriers were cutting minks close and fitted. Eventually, she stopped wearing it and went back to cloth coats. She and my father had moved back to New York and she had less patience than ever for shopping. And then she was sick and went to bed. One Thanksgiving she was too sick to come to the table. My mother loved Thanksgiving almost as much as she loved making a show of normal family life. I knew she was dying.

The months went by, and she hung on. In the hospital, then out, then back in. She was drugged, and wretchedly thin, and her throat was so dry, or so clogged with mucus, that I could not understand anything she tried to say to me. If I nodded at her as if I understood, she would become furious because she knew I hadn't; if I said, "What?" or, "I don't understand," she would become furious at the effort it would take to say it again. And I was furious, too, because

I was there for some kind of answer—what kind of answer? what was the question? I don't know, but I wanted one, a big one, and there was no chance of getting it. The Thorazine kept her quiet and groggy and hallucinating. When the nurse would bring in lunch, soft food, no salt allowed, she would look around almost brightly and say, "I think I'll take it in the living room." I would become so angry at her at moments like that, so impatient. I wanted to say, damn you, there is no living room, you're in a hospital, you're dying, you're going off without having explained any of it. And she would look up and open her mouth just slightly, and I would put another spoonful into it.

Then it was September. Fall. The room had a nice view of Gracie Mansion and the leaves were turning. It was a corner room on the sixth floor, which is, for those who care, a little like being seated at the right table. She did care. She managed, almost until the end, to keep up appearances. If the nurse was new, she would raise herself a bit, lift her arm in a dear and pathetic waft, and introduce us formally. "Miss Browning," she would say, "my daughter, Mrs. Greenburg." (My mother and the fish market were the only people who ever thought of me as Mrs. Greenburg.) Then she would collapse back onto the pillow and manage a bare flicker of a smile. I found it unbearable to be there and unbearable not to be there. I was conscious that I was going through an experience that writers write about, that I should be acutely aware of what was happening, but I hated that consciousness. And I could not look at her. She would moan with pain, and the nurse would reach under her, move her slightly, and the sheet would fall away and I would catch a glimpse of her legs, her beautiful legs now drained of muscle tone, gone to bones. The hallucinations went on. Then, one day, suddenly, she came into focus, knew exactly who I was, and like a witch, what I was thinking. "You're a reporter," she said to me. "Take notes."

Two days after she died, my sisters and I spent an afternoon—how to put this?—disposing of her possessions. It was an extremely odd day. People kept dropping in, somber people, to pay their respects to my father; in the bedroom were the four of us, not at all somber, relieved, really, that it was finally over, and finding a small and genuine pleasure in the trivial problem of what to do with her things.

Most of my mother's clothes were sent to charity. And the evening dresses, the beautiful chiffon Galanos dresses my father had bought her, were too big for any of us. But there was the mink. And there I was. The eldest. The most grown-up. It occurred to me I could cut it down to size or line another coat with it. Something. I took it.

A few weeks later, one of my sisters called. Did I take the mink? she asked. Yes. It's not fair, she said. She didn't even have a winter coat and I had hundreds and a big apartment and a rich husband and now I had the mink, too. You can have half of it, I said. She didn't want half of it. She didn't have the money for a winter coat much less the money to turn half a mink into something. What do you want? I said. She didn't know. There were three more phone calls, each uglier and more vituperative, thirty years of sibling rivalry come to a head over an eighteen-year-old mink. I have to make it clear that I was as awful as she was. I wanted the mink.

Finally, one day, we met in front of the Ritz Thrift Shop on Fifty-seventh Street. I was carrying the mink. She was barely speaking to me. We went inside, and a lady came over. We said we wanted to sell the mink. The lady took the fur in her hands and turned it over, peeling away the coat lining to look at the underside of the skins. She spent a good half second with it. "I won't give you a nickel for it," she said. The skins were worthless. Shot. Something like that. We walked out onto Fifty-seventh Street carrying the mink. It was suddenly a burden, a useless assemblage of old worn-out pelts. I didn't want it. She didn't want it. A year later, my maid asked for it and I gave it to her. Shortly thereafter, my maid's apartment was robbed and the burglar got the mink.

I will never have one. I know that now. And like a lot of things I will never have, I have mixed feelings about it. I mean, I could have one if I wanted one. I could squirrel away every extra nickel and buy myself, maybe not a perfect mink, but something made of mink noses or mink eyes or whatever spare parts make up that category of coats they call fun furs. But I don't really want one: a mink coat is serious, and I would have to change my life to go with it.

But I love her for having bought one. She had the only kind of mink worth having, the kind you pay for yourself. That is not the answer I was looking for, but it will have to do.

December, 1975

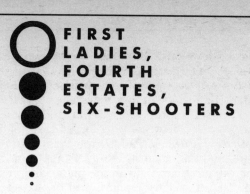

FIRST LADIES, FOURTH ESTATES, SIX-SHOOTERS

TOOK Margaret Trudeau's book with me on a trip to South Carolina the other day. Actually, it wasn't a bound book, it was a bunch of pages, and part of it got lost on the way back, and another part of it was spattered with barbecue sauce from Maurice Bessinger's Piggie Park Bar-B-Q and Drive-In Restaurant. When I got home and realized that the bottle of sauce had broken and that what was left of the book was stuck together with yellow goop and smelled like an old ham, I was secretly pleased. In fact, I have been secretly pleased at just about everything awful that has happened in connection with Margaret Trudeau since she gave up being first lady of Canada. I myself have always wanted to be first lady of the land—any land will do. And generally speaking, I feel that if I can't be first lady of the land, why should anyone else?

Margaret Trudeau is not really worth bothering about, of course. She is a disturbed, pathetic young woman who was in no way equipped to be the wife of a prime minister; she married a man who was apparently insensitive to her mental health and her immaturity and who, from all the evidence, was no use at all to her in her wretched attempts to cope. Ultimately, she had a nervous breakdown, which seems to have consisted primarily of wearing inappropriate clothes on state occasions. All of this ought to have made her an object of pity. But unfortunately, Mrs. Trudeau was also the consummate groupie; she was just bright enough to want to be famous for something more and just clever enough to hitch her separation from her husband to some empty feminist rhetoric about the price of being a political wife. Her book, *Beyond Reason* (Paddington Press, $10.95), is basically a compendium of this rhetoric, a long whine about life in a fishbowl and quarrels with the butler and gaffes at teatime and tiffs with security guards and the like. I am interested in it—though I am not particularly interested in her—because I'm not sure why women like this believe that they qualify for some sort of martyrdom.

What is so terrible, after all, about being first lady? It doesn't last forever, and while it does you don't have to have quarters for the washing machines. You never have to scrape the eggs off the bottom of the frying pan. You don't have to stand in the rain waiting for cabs or stand on line to get into movies you don't want to see because the movies you do want to see are already sold out. You can cut out a few areas of interest—abortion, I always thought, and beautiful stamps—and make a little trouble, even make a difference. Granted you might have to put in a long waiting period sitting home with young children while your husband is off on the campaign trail; it might take years before he is elected to the highest office. But there are many women in this country whose husbands are off on business a great deal of the time, and no one thinks they're entitled to become alcoholics or drug addicts or that it's somehow our fault if they end up in the loony bin. In any case, Margaret Trudeau didn't even have to wait; when she married Pierre Trudeau, she was twenty-two, and he was already prime minister.

She inherited two homes, a large staff, a considerable number of social obligations, and the chance to travel to foreign countries and meet the people who ran them. All this is described in *Beyond Reason* as a dreadful burden: The houses were badly decorated, and she had to battle for pale fabrics; the staff was ill-tempered, and she had to battle to get rid of them; the social obligations were tedious, and she had to battle to get out of them; the foreign countries provided too much security, and she had to battle to be on her own. Poor Margaret.

Eventually, after her breakdown, Mrs. Trudeau left her

husband with their three sons and went off to seek her fortune. Like many other rich young women who are newly single, she pretended for a time to be a photographer. She followed the Rolling Stones around and danced a lot in Studio 54. She attempted to become a movie star. The fact that the press reported her exploits as if they mattered and as if she were a rational being no doubt contributed to her belief in her own importance. Her book has been preceded by months of intense hints by her publishers that it would tell all. In it we learn that Mrs. Trudeau flirted with Fidel Castro, that Prince Charles looked down her dress, and that her husband did not believe in birth control and gave her a black eye after her weekend with the Rolling Stones. All this is pretty bland stuff. Apparently as a result, Mrs. Trudeau has in recent weeks taken to revealing the hot stuff she left out: the affair she claims to have had with Senator Ted Kennedy, for example, and her passionate sex with her husband following the black eye. These stories have been even more satisfying to me than the fate of my bottle of barbecue sauce because they serve to remind us that what Margaret Trudeau really knows about is not what happens to women who marry politicians but instead what happens to groupies who go too far. Groupies belong with third-string bass players and maybe an occasional lead guitarist, but they have no business with prime ministers. And vice versa, I might add.

May, 1979

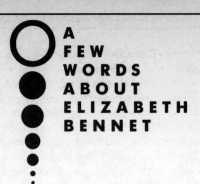

A FEW WORDS ABOUT ELIZABETH BENNET

HE other day they sent me a photograph of the actress who plays Miss Elizabeth Bennet in *Pride and Prejudice*, and I took one look at it and threw it into the garbage can. All things considered, this was a mild response. I have spent twenty years knowing exactly what Elizabeth Bennet looks like, and she does not look a bit like this person they have gotten to play her. She looks like me.

It has been possible for me to persist in this delusion as long as I have partly because I love Elizabeth Bennet and partly because Jane Austen, who created her, managed to leave out of her novel any detailed physical description of her heroine. She does write that Lizzy is not as beautiful as her sister Jane and that she has fine eyes—there's much made of those fine eyes—and a pleasant figure. But there is not a word about whether she is short or tall, blond or brunette; not a word about her nose or her lips; and while the fine eyes are said to be dark, there is not a word as to whether they are dark brown, or dark blue, or dark green, or dark lavender, or the color I happen to know them to be, which is dark hazel.

• • •

I fell in love with Elizabeth Bennet the first time I read *Pride and Prejudice*, and I have read the book at least once a year ever since. "It is a truth universally acknowledged," the book begins, "that a single man in possession of a good fortune must be in want of a wife." That glorious sentence is a threshold into Austen's world, a world of manners and domestic arrangements, a world where nothing—not politics nor war, which are simply not mentioned—is as important as the right match. Each time I cross into this world I bring to it the same intensity and sense of suspense I felt the first time through. I cannot put the book down. I am on tenterhooks about Elizabeth and Mr. Darcy. I am stunned by what becomes of Wickham. I am captivated by Elizabeth's father and appalled by her mother. I am furious at Miss Bingley. And when it becomes clear that things will work out, the lovers will triumph—when Elizabeth unexpectedly meets Mr. Darcy while walking through Pemberley and realizes his feelings for her are unchanged—I cry.

All this may say more about me and my rather dippy capacity for romance than it does about the book, but I doubt it: *Pride and Prejudice* is one of the greatest romantic comedies ever written, a novel about the possibility of love between equals, and in many ways it is the forerunner of a genre it was undoubtedly instrumental in creating. Two strong-willed people—one of them rich, the other not—meet and take an instant dislike to each other. She reacts by being arch and provocative; he is attracted by her audacity, her playfulness, her intellect, and, as Elizabeth reminds Mr. Darcy at the end of the book, her bad manners. "You may as well call it impertinence at once," she says. "The fact is that you were sick of civility, of deference, of officious attention. You were disgusted with the women who were always speaking and looking and thinking for *your* approbation alone." Eventually—after a long push and pull, half a dozen misunderstandings, and one explosive rejection—the lovers soften ever so slightly, acknowledge themselves to be possessed of at least one flaw apiece, and realize they were meant for each other, class distinctions aside.

What a lovely fantasy this plot is! It is the dream of any woman who has ever wanted to believe that what really matters is not beauty but brains, not flirtation but wit; it is the dream of every young woman who has ever been a wallflower. Indeed, when Elizabeth first meets Mr. Darcy, she is exactly that: She is sitting on the sidelines at a dance when she is pointed out to him, and to her amusement she hears his comment on her looks: "She is tolerable; but not handsome enough to tempt *me*; and I am in no humour at present to give consequence to young ladies who are slighted by other men." It is also the dream of every young woman who has ever worried she would never marry; for here the sister who is most serious, most thoughtful, most sensitive, is rewarded in the end by the very thing she has been shown to care least about—a rich husband. And for a moment—in spite of the many examples in Austen's work to the contrary—we are allowed to believe in the likelihood of a great marriage. "I know your disposition, Lizzy," Elizabeth's father tells her. "I know that you could be neither happy nor respectable unless you truly esteemed your husband, unless you looked up to him as a superior. Your lively talents would place you in the greatest danger in an unequal marriage. You could scarcely escape discredit and misery. My child, let me not have the grief of seeing *you* unable to respect your partner in life."

(The plot of *Pride and Prejudice* and the scrappy, feisty dialogue that characterizes Elizabeth and Mr. Darcy's relationship—the skittering banter, the deft back and forth—have been imitated in thousands of novels that have been written since and dozens of movies: *It Happened One Night*, with Claudette Colbert and Clark Gable; *The Lady Vanishes*, with Margaret Lockwood and Michael Redgrave; *Woman of the Year*, with Katharine Hepburn and Spencer Tracy. In these movies the convention is reversed: The part of the not-rich person is played by the man, and *he* is first to be arch and impertinent, *she* is the prideful snob. For the most perfect illustration of what might happen to an Elizabeth and a Mr. Darcy *after* they marry, see *The Thin Man*, with William Powell and Myrna Loy.)

I may be deluded about the similarity between Elizabeth Bennet's looks and mine, but I have never been as foolish on the question of character. Hers is far superior to mine. Her flaw is that she is too quick to form opinions based on first impressions; in short, that she is prejudiced. And that is her only flaw. I have at least a dozen as serious as that and a few far worse. The Austen character I most resemble, I am sorry to say, is not Elizabeth Bennet but Emma Woodhouse, of *Emma*. Now there's a woman with flaws: She's manipulative, bossy, and controlling. There are few Austen lovers who do not believe *Emma* to be Austen's finest work, but I have always been grumpy about it; it's too close to home. I prefer my literary heroines to be perfect, unlike me; and Lizzy is as close to perfect as she can be and still be interesting. In fact, I consider her flaw so minor that the first time I read *Pride and Prejudice* I assumed that both nouns in the title referred to Mr. Darcy. Who, after all, could blame Elizabeth for thinking ill of a man who insulted her at a dance? Who could think her genuinely prejudiced? Not I, that's who.

Recently, I was reading a novel by one of the most shrill of the feminist writers, who complained in it that there were no more Mr. Darcys. There are probably no more Elizabeth Bennets either. What's more, there were probably none in the first place. Which is wonderful. It means that those of us who would love to be like her can never feel too bad that we aren't; no one is. That's what makes Lizzy so lovable: She doesn't exist.

October, 1980

DOROTHY SCHIFF AND THE NEW YORK POST

I

FEEL bad about what I'm going to do here. What I'm going to do here is write something about Dorothy Schiff, and the reason I feel bad about it is that a few months ago, I managed to patch things up with her and now I'm going to blow it. She had been irritated with me for several years because I told the story about her and Otto Preminger's sauna on the radio, but we managed to get through a pleasant dinner recently, which made me happy—not because I care whether or not Dorothy Schiff is irritated with me but simply because I have a book coming out this summer, and if she were speaking to me, I might have a shot at some publicity in the *New York Post*. Ah, well. It's not easy being a media columnist. The publicity I had in mind, actually, was this little feature the *Post* runs on Saturdays called "At Home With," where semi-famous people tell their favorite recipes. Mine is beef borscht.

Dorothy Schiff is the publisher, editor and owner of the *New York Post*, America's largest-selling afternoon newspaper. I used to work there. The *Post* is a tabloid that has a smaller news hole than the *New York Daily News*—five front pages, various parts of which are often rented out to Chock Full o' Nuts and Lüchow's. It also has a center magazine section containing mostly *Washington Post* columnists, a first-rate sports section and drama critic, and Rose Franzblau, Earl Wilson and Dear Abby. It takes about eleven minutes to read the *Post*, and there are more than half a million New Yorkers like me who spend twenty cents six days a week to kill eleven minutes reading it. It is probably safe to say that fewer and fewer young people read the *Post*, and that fewer and fewer young people understand why anyone does. It is a terrible newspaper.

The reason it is, of course, is Dorothy Schiff. A great deal has been written about Mrs. Schiff in various places over the past years, and some of it—I'm thinking here of Gail Sheehy's article in *New York* at the end of 1973—has captured perfectly her coquettish giddiness, her penchant for trivia and her affection for gossip. It is taken for granted in these articles that Dolly Schiff is a very powerful woman—she is in fact very powerful for a woman and not particularly powerful for a newspaper publisher. What is rarely discussed is her product. In Sheehy's article, I suppose this was partly because Mrs. Schiff had manuscript approval, and partly because the publisher of *New York*, like so many other men Mrs. Schiff toys with, thinks that someday he will buy the *New York Post* from her. But it is a major omission: There is no other big-city newspaper in America that so perfectly reflects the attitudes and weaknesses of its owner. Dorothy Schiff has a right to run her paper any way she likes. She owns it. But it seems never to have crossed her mind that she might have a public obligation to produce a good newspaper. Gail Sheehy quite cleverly compared her with Scheherazade, but it would be more apt, I think, to compare her with Marie Antoinette. As in let them read schlock.

In 1963, when I went to work there as a reporter, the *New York Post* was located in a building on West Street, near the Battery. The first day I went there, I thought I had gotten out of the elevator in the fire exit. The hallway leading to the city room was black. Absolutely black. The smell of urine came wafting out of the men's room in the middle of the long hallway between the elevator and the city room. The glass door to the city room was filmed with dust, and written on it, with a finger, was the word "Philthy." The door was cleaned four years later, but the word remained; it had managed to erode itself onto the glass. Then, through the door, was the city room. Rows of desks jammed up against one another, headset phones, manual typewriters, stacks of copy paper, cigarette butts all over the floor—all of it pretty routine for a city room, albeit a city room of the 1920s. The problem was the equipment. The staff of the *Post* was small, but it was too large for the city room and for the number of chairs and desks and telephones in it. If you arrived at the *Post* five minutes late, there were no chairs left. You would go hunt one up elsewhere on the floor, drag it to an empty space, and then set off to find a phone. You cannot be a newspaper reporter without a phone. The phones at the *Post* were the old-fashioned headset type, with an earpiece-mouthpiece part that connected to a wire headpiece. Usually you could find the earpiece-mouthpiece part, but only occasionally was there a headpiece to go with it, which meant that you spent the day with your head cocked at a seventy-degree angle trying to balance this tiny phone against your shoulder as you typed. If you managed to assemble a complete telephone in the morning, it was necessary to lock it in your desk during lunch, or else it would end up on someone else's head for the afternoon. The trouble with that was that half the staff did not have desks, much less desk drawers to lock anything in.

None of this was supposed to matter. This was the newspaper business. You want air conditioning, go work at a newsmagazine. You want clean toilets, go work in advertising. Besides, there was still a real element of excitement to working at the *New York Post* in 1963. The paper had been a good paper once, when James Wechsler was the editor, and for a while it was possible to believe that it would be again. Mrs. Schiff had kicked Wechsler upstairs, had changed the focus of the paper from hard-hitting, investigative and left-wing to frothy, gossipy and women-oriented, but we all thought that would change eventually. At some point in the next few years, several New York papers would shut down. None of us really thought the *Post* would. "The most depressing thing about the *Post*," a reporter who once worked there used to say, "is that it will never shut down." When the other papers folded, the *Post* would have to get better. It would have to absorb the superior financial-page reporters from the other afternoon papers, the superior columnists from the *Herald Tribune*. It would have to run two more pages of news, enlarge its Washington bureau, beef up its foreign coverage, hire more staff, pay them better, stop skimping on expense accounts. Why I believed this

I don't know, but I believed it for years. The managing editor, Al Davis, who once dumped four gallons of ice water on my head in an attempt to tell me how he felt about the fact that I was leaving the *Post* for a while to go live in Europe, was fired in 1965, and we all had several months of euphoria thinking his replacement would make a difference. Blair Clark, the former CBS newsman and thread millionaire, came in as Mrs. Schiff's assistant—he too thought he would be able to buy the *Post* from her—and we all thought he would make a difference. The *Trib* folded, and the *Journal*, and the *World Journal Tribune*, and we all thought that would make a difference. Nothing made a difference.

I first met Mrs. Schiff a few weeks after I started working at the *Post*. I was summoned to lunch in her office, a privilege very few other reporters were granted in those days, and the reason for it had mainly to do with the fact that my parents were friends of her daughter, and I suspect she felt safe with me, thought I was of her class or some such. "You're so lucky to be working," she said to me at that meeting. "When I was your age, I never did anything but go to lunch." Mrs. Schiff's custom during these lunch meetings—perhaps as a consequence of spending so much of her youth in expensive restaurants at midday—was to serve a sandwich from the fly-strewn luncheonette on the ground floor of the *Post* building. A roast beef sandwich. Everyone who had lunch with her got a roast beef sandwich. Lyndon Johnson, Bobby Kennedy and me, to name a few. She thought it was very amusing of her, and I suppose it was. She would sit on one of her couches, looking wonderful-for-her-age—she is seventy-two now, and she still looks wonderful-for-her-age—and talk to whoever was on the other couch. There was, as far as I could tell, almost no way to have an actual conversation with her. She dominated, tantalized, sprinkled in little tidbits, skipped on to another topic. Once, I remember, she told me apropos of nothing that President Johnson had been up to see her the week before.

"Do you know what he told me?" she said.

"No," I said.

"He told me that Lady Bird fell down on the floor in a dead faint the other day, with her eyes bulging out of her head."

"Yes?" I said, thinking the story must go on to make a

point, to relate to whatever we'd just been talking about. But that was it.

In the course of that first meeting, I asked Mrs. Schiff a question, and her answer to it probably sums her up better than anything else she ever said to me. The newspaper strike was still on—she had walked out of the Publishers' Association a few weeks before and had resumed publication—and I was immensely curious about what went on during labor negotiations. I didn't know if the antagonists were rude or polite to one another. I didn't know if they said things like "I'll give you Mesopotamia if you'll give me Abyssinia." I asked her what it had been like. She thought for a moment and then answered. "Twenty-eight men," she said. "All on my side." She paused. "Well," she said, "I just ran out of things to wear."

That was Mrs. Schiff on the 114-day newspaper strike. She took everything personally, and at the most skittishly feminine personal level. There was always debate over what made her change her endorsement from Averell Harriman to Nelson Rockefeller in the 1958 gubernatorial election, but the only explanation I ever heard that made any sense was that a few days before the election, she went to a Harriman dinner and was left off the dais. She was obsessed with personal details, particularly with the medical histories of famous persons and the family lives of Jews who intermarried. I once spent two days on the telephone trying to check out a story she heard about Madame Nhu and a nervous breakdown ten years before, and I was constantly being ordered to call back people I had written profiles on in order to insert information about whether they were raising their children as Jews or Episcopalians or whatever.

Every little whim she had was catered to. Her yellow onionskin memos would come down from the fifteenth floor, and her editors, who operated under the delusion that their balls were in escrow, would dispatch reporters. In 1965, during the New York water shortage, she sent the one about Otto and the sauna. "Otto Preminger has added two floors to his house under my bedroom window," she wrote. "One, I understand, is for a movie projection room and the other, a sauna bath. Frequently, I hear water running for hours on end, from the direction of the Preminger house. It would be interesting to find out if a substantial amount of water is or is not required by such luxuries. Please investigate." The memo was given to me, and I spent the next day writing and then rewriting a memo to Mrs. Schiff explaining that saunas did not use running water. This did not satisfy her. So Joe Kahn, the *Post*'s only investigative reporter, was sent up to Lexington Avenue and Sixty-second Street to find the source of the sound of running water. He found nothing.

Ultimately, I discovered what union negotiations were like. I became a member of the grievance committee and the contract committee, and the head of the plant and safety committee. About the plant and safety committee—I was also the only member of it, and I think it is accurate to say that everyone at the *Post* thought I was crazy even to care. It wasn't precisely a matter of caring, though. I was physically revolted by the conditions at the newspaper, none of which had changed at all since I began there. The entrance to the lobby was still black, Philthy and the dust were still on the door, and there was a slowly accumulating layer of soot all over the city room. Then there were the bathrooms. They were cleaned only once a day and had overflowing waste-baskets and toilets. The men's room in the entrance hall still had no door, and there was something wrong with the uri-nals. In the summertime, it was especially unpleasant to walk past it.

I first began to bring up my complaints about plant con-ditions to management in the grievance committee. Mrs. Schiff was not present. I asked that the hallway be painted. I asked for a snap lock on the men's room door. I asked for more chairs and phones in the city room. I asked if it were possible to hire a few more maintenance people—there was one poor man whose job consisted of cleaning all the bath-rooms and of sweeping out the city room each day. Nothing happened. About a year after I began to complain, I was summoned to lunch again by Mrs. Schiff because of a mem-orandum I had written about Betty Friedan. I asked her about the possibility of cleaning the city room and repainting the entrance, and she looked at me as if the idea had never occurred to her. (The next week, the hallway was in fact painted and the city room cleaned for the first time in four years.) Then I mentioned the bathrooms, which she referred to for the rest of the conversation as the commodes. She listened to me—as just about everyone did—as if I were addled, and then said that she didn't really see the point of keeping the commodes clean because her employees were the kind of people who were incapable of not dirtying them up. I tried to explain to her that if the plant were clean, her employees would not be careless about dirtying it. I suggested that she had exactly the same sort of people working for her as there were at the *Daily News*, and the bathrooms at the *Daily News* looked fine. I don't think she understood a word I said.

One more thing about that lunch. We were talking about Betty Friedan. I had written a memo about an article she had written for the magazine section of the Sunday *Herald Tribune*; I thought we could develop a series about women in New York from it. The memo had been sent up to Mrs. Schiff, who wanted to talk about it. It turned out that she was upset with Betty Friedan and seemed to think that *The Feminine Mystique* had caused her daughter, a Beverly Hills housewife, to leave her household and spend a lot of money becoming a California politician. Mrs. Schiff thought I wanted to write a put-down of Mrs. Friedan—which was fine with her. I explained that that wasn't what I had in mind at all; I agreed with Betty Friedan, I said. "For example," I said, reaching for something I hoped Mrs. Schiff would understand, "Betty Friedan writes that housewives with nothing else to do often put a great deal of nagging pressure on their husbands to earn more money so they can buy bigger cars and houses."

Mrs. Schiff thought it over. "Yes," she said. "I've often thought that was why the men around here ask for raises as much as they do."

Top pay for reporters at that time was around ten thousand dollars a year. Mrs. Schiff had no idea that it took more than that to raise a family. She had no idea how the people who worked for her lived. She did not know that one hundred dollars was not a generous Christmas bonus. She did not even have a kind of noblesse oblige. She just sat up there serving roast beef sandwiches and being silly.

Jack Newfield, another *New York Post* alumnus, wrote an article about the paper in 1969 for *Harper's*, and in it he quoted Blair Clark, who was then assistant publisher of the *Post* for a brief interlude. "Dolly's problem," said Clark, "is that her formative experience was the brutal competitive situation the *Post* used to be in. She doesn't know how to make it a class newspaper." In the lean years, she survived by cutting overhead, keeping the staff small, cutting down on out-of-town assignments, paying her employees as little as possible. And all this still goes on, not just because she still thinks she is in a competitive situation but also because she survived, and she did it her way. She did it by being stingy; and she did it by being frothy and giddy; she was vindicated and she sees no reason to do things differently.

The last time I saw her, she mentioned that she had heard the things I said about her on the radio. "Nora," she said to me, "you know perfectly well you learned a great deal at the *Post*." But of course I did. I even loved working there. But that's not the point. The point is the product.

Nora Ephron's Beef Borscht

Put 3 pounds of beef chuck cut for stew and a couple of soupbones into a large pot. Add 2 onions, quartered, and 6 cups beef broth and bring to a boil, simmering 15 minutes and skimming off the scum. Add 2 cups tomato juice, the juice from a 1-pound can of julienne beets, salt, pepper, the juice of 1 lemon, 1 tablespoon cider vinegar, 2 tablespoons brown sugar, and bring to a boil. Then simmer slowly for 2½ hours until the beef is tender. Add the beets left over from the beet juice, and another can of beets and juice. Serve with huge amounts of sour cream, chopped dill, boiled potatoes and pumpernickel bread. Serves six.

April, 1975

THE PALM BEACH SOCIAL PICTORIAL

I **AM** sitting here thinking a mundane thought, which is that one picture is worth a thousand words. The reason I am sitting here thinking this is that I am looking at one picture, a picture of someone named Mignon Roscher Gardner on the cover of the *Palm Beach Social Pictorial*, and I cannot think how to describe it to you, how to convey the feeling I get from looking at this picture and in fact every other full-color picture that has ever appeared on the cover of this publication.

The *Palm Beach Social Pictorial* appears weekly throughout the winter season in Palm Beach and I get it in the mail because a friend of mine named Liz Smith writes a column in it and has it sent to me. There are several dozen of us on Liz Smith's list, and I think it is safe to say that we all believe that the *Palm Beach Social Pictorial* is the most wonderful publication in America. Beyond that, each of us is very nearly obsessed with the people in it. My particular obsession is Mignon Roscher Gardner, but from time to time I am un-faithful to her, and I get involved instead with the life of Anky Von Boythan Revson Johnson, who seems to live in a turban, or Mrs. Woolworth Donahue, who apparently never goes anywhere without her two Great Danes nuzzling her lap. One friend of mine is so taken with Helene (Mrs. Roy)

Tuchbreiter and her goo-goo-googly eyes that he once made an entire collage of pictures of her face.

Mignon Roscher Gardner, who happens to be a painter of indeterminate age and platinum-blond hair, has appeared on the cover of the *Pictorial* twice in the last year, both times decked in ostrich feathers. Anyone who appears on the cover of the *Pictorial* pays a nominal sum to do so; Mrs. Gardner's appearances usually coincide with an opening of her paintings in Palm Beach, although the last one merely coincided with the completion of her portrait of Dr. Josephine E. Raeppel, librarian emeritus of Albright College in Reading, Pennsylvania. Most of the painters whose work appears on the cover of the *Pictorial* are referred to as "famed, international" painters, but Mrs. Gardner is a local, and the furthest the *Pictorial* will go in the famed-international department is to call her prominent. "Prominent artist-aviatrix," for example—that's what they called her last February, when she appeared on the cover in her hair and turquoise ostrich feathers along with a painting from a new series she called "The Cosmobreds." The painting was of a naked young man on a flying black horse, and according to the *Pictorial*, it was a departure from her usual work in animals and sailboats and portraits because "Mignon wanted to combine her love for horses and for flying." In back of the painting of the Cosmobred and Mrs. Gardner herself are some curtains, and if you ask me, they're the highlight of the photograph. They are plain white curtains, but the valances are covered with chintz daisies, and the curtains are trimmed, but heavily trimmed, with yellow and green pompons, the kind drum majorettes trim their skirts and boots with.

Inside the *Palm Beach Social Pictorial* are advertisements ("Dress up your diamond bracelet"), columns and pictures. The pictures show the people of Palm Beach eating lunch, wearing diamonds in the daytime, eating dinner, attending charity functions, and wearing party clothes. Most of the people are old, except that some of the women have young husbands. It is apparently all right to have a young husband if you are an old woman in Palm Beach, but not vice versa; in fact, the vice versa is one of the few things the columnists in the *Social Pictorial* get really upset about. Here, for instance, is columnist Doris Lilly writing about the guests at a recent party she attended: "Bill Carter (now U.N. ambassador to U.N.I.C.E.F.) proved he really does love children by bringing his latest airline hostess." And here from another columnist, Maria Durell Stone, is another guest list: "Then there were the Enrique Rousseaus, she's Lilly Pulitzer, and even Lilly's ex, Peter, was there with, well, as someone said, 'I don't think it's his daughter but she just might be.'" Every so often, the *Pictorial* prints pictures of people they describe as members of Palm Beach's Younger Set; they all look to be in their mid-forties.

There are two types of columnists who write for the *Pictorial*—locals, and correspondents from elsewhere. There are two advantages to being a correspondent from elsewhere: You don't have to spend the winter in Palm Beach, and you get a lofty title on the masthead. Wally Cedar, who writes from Beverly Hills and Acapulco, is the *Pictorial*'s International Editor, and Liz Smith, who writes from New York, is the National Editor. With one exception—and I'll get to her in a minute: she's Maria Durell Stone—the local columnists in the *Pictorial* have tended to be relentlessly cheerful women whose only quibbles about life in Palm Beach have to do with things like the inefficiency of the streetlights on Worth Avenue. Cicely Dawson, who owns the *Pictorial* along with her husband Ed, whom she always refers to as "our better half," writes a goings-on-about-town column in which she manages to summon unending enthusiasm and exclamation points for boutiques, galleries, parties, and new savings banks in town. "Congratulations to Nan and James Egan of the James Beauty Salon on their recent twenty-fifth anniversary," Dawson once wrote. "No client would guess from the cheerful attitude of this wonderful couple what hardship they have had these past few months. After an illness-free life, James was diagnosed as having chronic kidney failure last December. Oh that Palm Beach County had an Artificial Kidney Center!...because that's what James needs."

In all fairness, Mrs. Dawson is almost a grouch in comparison to Leone "Call Me the Pollyanna of Palm Beach" King, who until her retirement in 1973 could not find enough good things to say about the place. "Where else," Mrs. King once asked in a long series of rhetorical questions, "could you find families offering living quarters to people of low incomes, without at least making some sort of charge? ...Where could you find friends with splendid flower gardens leaving a message with their gardeners to send certain people bouquets during the winter while they are off on a trip around the world? Where could you find big bags of fruit from a Palm Beach orange grove on your doorstep at regular intervals? ... Don't let fabulously rich people throw you. They are just the same as anyone else except that they can do what they jolly well please when they jolly well please. They have likes and dislikes, aches and pains, problems. They are just people."

Maria Durell Stone has left the *Palm Beach Social Pictorial*— she has been stolen away by the West Palm Beach daily paper—but her two years on the weekly coincided, and not coincidentally either, with what I think of as the *Pictorial*'s Golden Era, so I cannot leave her out of this. Mrs. Stone is a Latin-looking lady with a tremendous amount of jet-black hair who is divorced from architect Edward Durell Stone and has taken not one but two of his names along with her. She began writing for the *Pictorial* three years ago, and no one writing in any of the Palm Beach publications comes near her gift for telling it like it is. "I've done nothing but praise the Poinciana Club since it opened," she wrote last year, "but being a critic means that every now and then one must speak the truth and I am sorry to say it, but Bavarian Night there was a disaster."

Mrs. Stone's main problem in life—and the theme of her column too—had to do with being a single woman in a place where there are few eligible men. There are a lot of us with this problem, God knows, but she managed to be more in touch with it than anyone I know. Not a column passed without a pointed remark to remind the reader that this Mrs. Stone was looking for a Roman spring. "I met Vassili Lambrinos this week and he's divine," she wrote one week. "Dorothy Dodson, petite, refreshing and vivacious, gave a luncheon for him and I got to know him better—unfortunately not as much as I would like to, but what's a poor bachelor girl to do?" Another week, Mrs. Stone went to a charity auction: "There were numerous items to bid on and I did covet that stateroom for two on the *S.S. France*, but as luck would have it, someone else got it. I wouldn't have known who to take with me anyway, so it's probably just as well." Age was no barrier: "One of the best things of the evening," she wrote of the Boys' Club Dinner, "was the Boys' Club Chorus, which consisted of adorable little boys of unfortunate circumstances who sang many lively numbers at the top of their divine adolescent voices. It was heartwarming to hear." Apparently, Mrs. Stone's subtlety was not lost on her readers: "Stanton Griffis, that amazing ex-ambassador who sat next to me at the Salvation Army luncheon the other day, told me that if I really wanted to get the right man, I should put an ad in my column saying, 'Wanted: Intelligent, handsome, lean, tall, romantic type with kindness and money.' Well, now that I've said it, let's see if my octogenarian friend is right."

From time to time, something sneaks into the *Pictorial* that has to do with the outside world, and when it does, it is usually in Liz Smith's column. Miss Smith writes for the publication as if she were addressing a group of—well, a group of people who winter in Palm Beach. She interrupts her column of easygoing gossip and quotes to bring her readers little chautauquas; last year's were about Richard Nixon ("Hope all you people who couldn't stomach poor old Hubert are happy these days," one of them concluded) and this year's are about oil and the Middle East. ("So here are the most fascinating and frightening statistics I've read recently, from *The New Republic*. You remember *The New Republic*—it's liberal, left, and riddled with integrity, but even so, don't ignore the statistics.")

The rich are different from you and me; we all know that even if some of the people in Palm Beach don't. But it is impossible to read the *Social Pictorial* without suspecting that the rich in Palm Beach are even more different. One of my friends tells me that Palm Beach used to be a rather nice place and that now it's become a parody of itself; I don't know if she's right, but if she is, the *Social Pictorial* reflects this perfectly. If there were more communities like it, I don't think I would find the *Palm Beach Social Pictorial* so amusing. But there aren't, so I do.

The *Palm Beach Social Pictorial*, P.O. Box 591, Palm Beach, Florida. By subscription $10 a year.

May, 1975

RICHARD COLLIN AND THE SPAGHETTI RECIPE

IT is generally agreed among the people who have any perspective on it at all—and there are only a handful who do—that the entire civic scandal of Richard Collin and the mysterious spaghetti sauce recipe could only have happened in New Orleans—which was, in fact, where it did happen—and for fairly obvious reasons. For one thing, New Orleans is one of the two most ingrown, self-obsessed little cities in the United States. (The other is San Francisco.) For another, people in New Orleans really care about food, care about it passionately, can spend hours arguing over whether Antoine's is better than Galatoire's or the other way a-round. What sets the people of New Orleans apart from the people of San Francisco in this respect is that in New Orleans, there is basically nothing to do but eat and then argue about it.

All of which should have made Richard Collin a welcome addition to the New Orleans food scene. Richard Collin is a restaurant critic. He is New Orleans's first and only serious restaurant critic. A professor of American history at the University of New Orleans, Collin, forty-three, began his career in food in 1970 as the author of *The New Orleans Underground Gourmet* (Simon and Schuster). A few months after its publication he was hired by the *New Orleans States-*

Item to write a weekly restaurant column. In it, Collin employs an extremely elaborate system of stars and dots and parentheses and *X*'s which takes over five column-inches of space to explain each week. In addition, he uses an expression he coined to describe things he particularly loves; he calls them platonic dishes. "This is my own personal accolade," Collin once explained. "The term is derived from Plato's *Republic*. It simply means the best imaginable realization of a particular dish." Collin's style of criticism can best be described as hyperbolic; it can also be described as self-important and longwinded. But he works hard, and his guidebook is considered as reliable as any city restaurant guide in the country.

In New Orleans, however, the question of whether Collin is reliable is not the point. The point is that he is critical—and in public. Arguing privately about the merits of various restaurants is one thing, but criticizing them publicly runs completely counter to the local spirit of boosterism. To make matters worse, Collin is not even from New Orleans; he is from Philadelphia and he is seen as an outsider who has stumbled onto a gold mine at the expense of local merchants. So when the episode of the spaghetti sauce recipe and the two thousand dollars surfaced a few months ago, the city fathers fell upon it as an excuse to ask the *States-Item* to investigate Collin. But I'm getting ahead of the story.

The position of restaurant critic is a new slot at most newspapers; nonetheless, the job has a tradition and a set of ethics. The classic American restaurant critic is rarely photographed, makes reservations under a pseudonym, cannot accept free meals, and never reveals his identity to a proprietor. Some restaurant critics have gone to extraordinary lengths to preserve their anonymity; last year, for example, Jack Shelton of *San Francisco* magazine was subpoenaed to testify in a local trial, and he appeared wearing a mask.

Prior to the publication of his book, Richard Collin followed traditional practices; in any case, it would have done him no good to reveal himself, since his name meant nothing. But the success of the book, the newspaper column (which ran a sketch of Collin alongside his by-line) and subsequent public appearances made Collin's face and name well-known. By 1973, when the revised edition of *The Underground Gourmet* was published, Collin had moved into a slightly revisionist phase of behavior. He continued to pay for his meals, but he admitted that from time to time a restaurateur managed to force a free one on him. He continued to reserve under a pseudonym, but it became increasingly difficult to keep from being recognized. He began to metamorphose into a role he thought of as a kindly godfather, but which might more correctly be defined as participatory journalist. He became a close friend of Warren Le Ruth, whose restaurant, Le Ruth's, received Collin's highest rating: four stars and ten platonic dishes. He gave advice to owners and to chefs. He seemed to regard himself as an impresario who was going to bring to New Orleans cuisine the acclaim it deserved. "I frequently introduce myself *after* the check has been paid," he wrote, "especially in smaller restaurants that are doing well and that deserve to be encouraged. I also notify restaurants in advance when a favorable review is to appear in the Saturday paper so that the restaurant does not run out of food by six or seven in the evening, as has happened when the pending review was kept a secret. For this edition I have not been quite as anonymous as I was for the first edition. Many restaurateurs saw me on television or met me at speaking engagements around town. However, known or unknown, distant or friendly, I have continued to base my evaluations solely on the genuine merits of the food restaurants serve. I enjoy being a restaurant critic too much to allow my integrity to be compromised."

The trouble began in April, 1973, with what looked—to Richard Collin, at least—like a pure case of civic duty. Turci's Original Italian Restaurant was about to close. Turci's was a typical grubby neighborhood restaurant on Poydras Street in downtown New Orleans; it had sluggish service but a platonic spaghetti sauce. It also had a platonic veal parmigiana, but the important thing was the spaghetti sauce: it had a rich, tomatoey, almost burned flavor, and it was packed with meatballs, mushrooms and chicken. Collin had given the restaurant three stars and, with his customary enthusiasm, announced that Turci's cooking was "unsurpassed in New Orleans or in Italy itself." But times got hard for Turci's, the neighborhood changed, and Rose Turci Serwich, the daughter of the original owners, decided she would have to shut down. Collin heard the news and wrote a column suggesting that someone raise the money to move Turci's to a better location and save the restaurant.

A New Orleans businessman named Joe Bernstein read the article. Along with two partners, he had just bought a building on Magazine Street and was looking for a ground-floor tenant. Bernstein called one of his partners, Ben C. Toledano, who occasionally wrote book reviews for the *States-Item* and knew Collin; Toledano called Collin and asked him to serve as intermediary in arranging the purchase of Turci's. "It was an uncomfortable position," Collin recalled recently, "but it was part of my responsibility to the community at large." Collin went ahead and arranged for Turci's to sell its name and good will for a reported ten thousand dollars and for Mrs. Serwich to sign an employment contract. A year later, the new Turci's opened. It was beautiful. It was crowded. It was fashionable. And it was terrible. Everyone knew it—Joe Bernstein knew it and Mrs. Serwich knew it. Both of them were on the phone to Richard Collin to complain about restaurant personnel. Mrs. Serwich hated the chef. Mrs. Serwich had objections to the manager. Joe Bernstein was going crazy because of the tension between Mrs. Serwich and the chef and Mrs. Serwich and the manager. But most of all, there was the problem of the spaghetti sauce. "I couldn't go to a cocktail party or go out on the street without someone telling me the sauce just wasn't the same," Joe Bernstein recalled. "I became frantic." The problem with the spaghetti sauce was really a very simple one: there was no recipe for it, and there never had been. The old Turci's spaghetti sauce had been a concoction made of tomato paste and leftovers. The new Turci's had no leftovers, owing to a streamlined kitchen and cost accounting; the new chef had no idea what to do under the circumstances. In the midst of all this, Richard Collin dropped in to Turci's for dinner.

The next day, he called Bernstein and told him to come by his house immediately. Bernstein arrived within a few minutes, and the first thing Collin asked him to do was to sign a release absolving Collin of any responsibility for what he was about to say. Bernstein signed and Collin began talking. He told Bernstein to fix the spaghetti sauce, eliminate the crab claws from the menu, and do something about the chef, who, Collin said, was "a Massachusetts Greek who didn't know from Turci's." If Bernstein failed to make improvements, Collin said he would be forced to give the restaurant a bad review—which he had in fact already written, and he read a few sample sentences from a piece of paper: "Frankly, we would all have been better off last year had the real Turci's been allowed to die a natural though unwelcome death. . . . It seems to me that in the move uptown what the new Turci's has proven is that one can turn a silk purse into a sow's ear. Requiescat." Within a few days, the chef quit—Bernstein says it had nothing to do with Collin's ultimatum—and Collin returned to the restaurant for a review. He gave the new Turci's three stars. "Try finding the likes of Turci's even in Italy," he wrote. "The new Turci's has the setting this marvelous restaurant has always deserved—a splendid place in which to serve its grand food. . . ."

At this point, we must pause to introduce a new character in this drama, a person Collin refers to as "my own favorite platonic dish." Rima Drell Reck Collin is a professor of comparative literature at the University of New Orleans, an editor of *The Southern Review*, and, according to her husband, "the most creative and gifted cook in the world now." She had just finished writing a New Orleans cookbook with her husband and was planning to open a food consulting firm in partnership with Warren Le Ruth of four-star, ten-platonic-dish fame. "The firm," says Collin, "was an attempt to get her out from being Mrs. Underground Gourmet. She's got enormous talent, but in this town she is still Mrs. Underground Gourmet."

One day a few weeks after the good review appeared, Joe Bernstein visited Richard and Rima Collin to talk about the restaurant. He was still concerned about its inconsistency, particularly when it came to the spaghetti sauce. One thing led to another, and before the session was up, Bernstein had hired Mrs. Collin's firm to fix the sauce. Bernstein paid her two thousand dollars for two months' work—after which time she and Le Ruth, who had not been able to implement a new recipe, fought with each other and dissolved the partnership. The next month, Mrs. Collin sent Bernstein another bill, which Bernstein refused to pay. There was considerable shouting on Bernstein's part and considerable crying on Mrs. Collin's part. According to Bernstein, Mrs. Collin threatened his bookkeeper and said that if he did not pay up, the restaurant would be hurt. Bernstein did not pay.

It was at this point, Richard Collin says, that he realized

for the first time that he was in a spot. "I was in a very bad situation," he said. "It was okay as far as helping the restaurant and shaking out the sauce—that struck me as a civic restoration—but once a falling-out occurred, I knew that anytime I changed the rating it would look suspect." In January, 1975, just before the Super Bowl, Collin nonetheless printed a revised set of ratings for New Orleans restaurants. Turci's was stripped down to an altogether new category— a star within parentheses, meaning "some good food but not a recommended restaurant." What intrigued the owners of Turci's about this new rating was that Collin had not eaten in Turci's at any time since his original review had appeared.

A month later, *Figaro*, a small New Orleans weekly newspaper (in which, in keeping with the tenor of this saga, Joe Bernstein's children own a minority interest), broke the story. *Figaro*'s editor, James Glassman, quoted Bernstein and Collin on the Turci's episode, and also quoted Chris Ansel, the owner of Christian's Restaurant, who said that Collin told him to fire his chef and cut down on the salt; when the chef failed to do so, Collin stripped Ansel of his stars and eleven platonic dishes. The *Figaro* article caused a sensation. The New Orleans Restaurant Association wrote the *States-Item* demanding that Collin be investigated. The Louisiana chefs association seconded the motion. A group of local restaurateurs tried to pressure the National Restaurant Association to drop Collin from a panel discussion at the association's annual convention. There were television debates. There was an acrimonious press conference. Mrs. Galatoire of Galatoire's accused Collin of not ordering a dish he subsequently reviewed. The *New Orleans Times-Picayune*— which has an active rivalry with the *States-Item* although both are owned by the Newhouse chain—unleashed its food writer to attack Collin.

Eventually, of course, the furor died down. The editor of the *States-Item* admitted that Collin had been "indiscreet" and that some of his behavior bordered on "a conflict of interest." The *Times-Picayune* food writer announced that he would write a rival restaurant guide in which no restaurant would receive an unfavorable rating. Bernstein, not having managed to formulate the spaghetti sauce, moved on to specialize in canneloni. The people of New Orleans settled down to dinner. And Richard Collin learned a lesson. Not the exact lesson he might have—about the function of a critic, for example, or about the limits of critical involvement, or about the ethics of critical behavior—but he did learn something. "I learned," he said, "that restaurants have a limited lifespan, and there's no point in trying to save them."

September, 1975

MY COUSIN ARTHUR IS YOUR UNCLE ART

THE other day, my sister Delia went up to the Bronx to buy a carpet from my cousin Arthur. I had last seen my cousin Arthur in 1963, when I went up to the Bronx to buy a carpet from my uncle Charlie, who is Cousin Arthur's father. Uncle Charlie and Cousin Arthur used to be in the carpet business together, but Cousin Arthur left the family business some years ago to go off on his own, largely because he did not get along with Cousin Norman, who was also in the family business and whom no one in the family gets along with except for Uncle Charlie, who gets along with everyone. Anyway, when my sister Delia came back from the Bronx, having bought a very nice carpet at a very good price, she called up.

"Guess who Cousin Arthur is?" she said.

"I give up," I said.

"Cousin Arthur is Uncle Art," she said.

Actually, as I later found out, Cousin Arthur is Uncle Art only some of the time; the rest of the time a person named Jeremiah Morris is Uncle Art, and that is part of the problem. Still, Cousin Arthur is Uncle Art more than Jeremiah Morris is Uncle Art, and if you don't know who Uncle Art is, that's either because you haven't had to buy a discount carpet in

New York lately, or because you're not in the carpet business. Uncle Art is to the carpet business what Frank Perdue is to the chicken business: in short, he has his own commercial.

"My name is Art Ephron," read the first of Cousin Arthur's Uncle Art advertisements, which ran, along with a large picture of Cousin Arthur himself, in the *New York Daily News* in 1972, "and I've been in the carpet business for, oh, longer than I care to remember. And every few weeks it seemed one of my relatives would say, 'Uncle Art, I was wondering, well, uh, maybe you could get us a break on some carpet. You know, something *nice*. Cheap.' So, one night, I was thinking. If I could do this for my relatives, why not for everybody?" The ad went on at some length, spelling out the special things about Cousin Arthur's Redi-Cut Carpets outlets (coffee, no pushy salesmen, a money-back guarantee, free rug cutting), and it ended with what has become the chain's slogan: "It's like having an uncle in the carpet business."

I was so stunned to discover that one of those people you see pitching their products on late-night television was a relative of mine that I promptly went up to the Bronx to see Cousin Arthur for myself. I found him on Webster Avenue, at one of his stores, and he turned out to be an extremely affable man. He was also, incidentally, the largest Ephron I have ever met (he is six feet tall and weighs two hundred ten pounds) and the only member of the family I know of who has a beard (although I haven't seen my cousin Erwin lately, and for all I know he may have one too). In any event, we went out to lunch and he told me about his advertising campaign.

"I started this company in 1971," Cousin Arthur began. "I'd been living in Detroit, working in the carpet business, and I felt that carpet retailing was ripe for a plain, pipe-rack approach, sort of like Robert Hall. I'd had a run with regular carpet retailing. I'd worked for Korvettes...."

"Is it true," I asked, "that E. J. Korvettes stands for Eight Jewish Korean War Veterans?"

"It's a base canard," said Cousin Arthur. "The 'E' is for Eugene Ferkauf, the 'J' is for Joe Zwillenberg, and Korvette is the name of a subchaser in World War Two. To get back to what I was saying, I thought there was room for a no-frills approach to carpet retailing with remnants, so I called my friend Lenny, and he found a location in Mount Vernon, and we opened up. We hired a small ad agency in Scarsdale, and they came up with an ad that read: 'Redi-Cut Carpets, a nice place to buy.' We stayed with them for about a year. The business was growing, but we weren't getting results from the ads. I'm a great advertising critic, but I can't create an ad from scratch. So I called Cousin Mike and asked him what to do." Cousin Michael Ephron is media director of Scali, McCabe, Sloves, the agency that created the Frank Perdue ad; he and Cousin Arthur had recently become friends on account of a carpet Michael needed for his den. "Michael didn't want the account for his agency," Arthur went on. "Big agencies hate handling retail ads. The detail work is incredible." Michael suggested that Arthur and his partner Len Stanger go see a small creative agency called Kurtz & Symon. "They made a presentation," said Arthur, "and we got married."

Kurtz & Symon went to work and came up with the Uncle Art ads; in addition, the agency had Uncle buttons printed for all the salesmen at Redi-Cut. Even Cousin Arthur's wife, Hazel, got a button that said Uncle Hazel. The ads worked. Pictures of Cousin Arthur as Uncle Art filled New York and Westchester County papers. Business got better. More branches were opened. And Kurtz & Symon began to press Cousin Arthur to take his advertising campaign to television. At the time, a man named Jerry Rosenberg, proprietor of J.G.E. Enterprises, a discount appliance store in Queens, had become a household word in New York because of his commercial, delivered in an unrelenting Brooklyn accent, that began: "So what's the story, Jerry?" It was logical for Cousin Arthur to go on television too. But it didn't work out that way.

"I got scared," said Cousin Arthur. "I'm no actor. I'm impatient. I'd gotten really annoyed with the amount of time it took just to do the print ads. They were doing these photo sessions of me where they roped off half the Mount Vernon store for two and a half hours just to take a picture. I was losing business. I was going crazy. And I didn't think I'd be any good on television. Lenny could have done it. Lenny's a real ham. Maybe the campaign should have been Uncle Len. But I didn't think I could do it. Suppose I blew it? So I said, Let's get a professional guy. They got an actor named Jeremiah Morris. Jerry's about five inches shorter than me, ten years older, he's bald and has no beard. Outside of that, he looks exactly like me."

Kurtz & Symon brought Morris and a toupee and a false beard up to the store to shoot the commercials. "I'm Uncle Art from Redi-Cut Carpets," Morris began, and Cousin Arthur became upset. He began to complain to both Don Kurtz and Jim Symon. "He kept trying to change the actor's performance," said Jim Symon, who I spoke to about all this. "Most of his complaints had to do with the fact that he, Arthur, was more handsome than the actor, and that he, Arthur, was taller. Then we showed him the ad when it was done and he complained some more. He said the actor was playing it too much like Jerry of J.G.E. By that time there was so much money committed to the ad it had to be run. It was an academic discussion."

A few weeks later, in the fall of 1973, the commercials went on the air. Cousin Arthur would sit in front of his television set, switching from one non-network channel to the next, watching Jeremiah Morris come on as Uncle Art six times a night. "I would look and listen and I would sort of resent the fact that he really didn't look or sound like me. It really began to bother me." Every so often, he would make his wife, Uncle Hazel, sit through yet another viewing of the commercial. "After it was over, I'd ask her, 'Do I really sound like that? Do I really look like that?' She'd say no. But everyone else thought I did. I began getting calls from people I'd known for years. 'I saw you on TV last night,' they'd say. No one ever said to me, 'Hey, that wasn't you.' Tell me. You've seen the commercial. Does that look like me? Does that sound like me?"

In fact, it doesn't. But in any case, the commercials worked. Soon there were four of them on television, and soon Cousin Arthur and his partner Lenny owned eight carpet outlets. Cousin Arthur could hardly complain. Or could he?

"There's something I think I should tell you," he said, lowering his voice so that no one in the Red Coach Grill at the Cross County Shopping Center could hear. "I think I'm getting a divorce from Kurtz and Symon."

"What?" I said.

"I'm thinking of dropping them and going absolutely gigantically big into radio."

"Why?"

"I spend thirty percent of my budget on agency fees," said

Cousin Arthur. "On radio you spend nothing. The radio station writes the ad for you. And my selling will be done by disk jockeys like Bob Grant, William B. Williams and Julius LaRosa."

"But what will happen to Uncle Art?" I asked.

"That's a problem," said Cousin Arthur. "We may be at the crossroads for Uncle Art."

"Have you talked to Cousin Michael about all of this?" I asked.

"No," said Cousin Arthur.

"I think you should," I said. "I think what all this is really about is that you wish you'd done the commercial yourself."

"I do wish I'd done it," said Cousin Arthur. "I can't get angry at anyone about it, though. I could have done it. It was my fault I didn't. But you want to know a thing I really regret? I had a chance to be head of a giant record company once. That I really regret. For five hundred dollars I could have owned twenty-five percent of Elektra Records. You know why I didn't?"

"Why?"

"My father talked me out of it."

That didn't surprise me. Thirty years ago Cousin Arthur's father, who you may recall is my uncle Charlie, told my parents it was a good thing they were selling their house on Turtle Bay in Manhattan, because the United Nations was being built and property values in the neighborhood were going to drop.

Cousin Arthur shook his head. "I should have done the ad," he said. "It would have been a thrill to see myself on television. Let's be honest about it. Everyone wants to be recognized."

"But you *are* recognized," I said.

"Only by family and friends," said Cousin Arthur.

"That's not true," I said. "My sister Delia's cabdriver recognized you."

"What did he say?" said Cousin Arthur.

"He said, 'Isn't that guy on TV?'"

"That's what I mean," said Cousin Arthur. "That's not really being recognized."

May, 1976

UPSTAIRS, DOWNSTAIRS

MY friend Kenny does not feel as bad about the death of Hazel as I do. My friend Ann has been upset about it for days. My friend Martha is actually glad Hazel is dead. I cried when Hazel died, but only for a few seconds, partly because I wasn't at all surprised. About three months ago, someone told me she was going to die, and since then I have watched every show expecting it to be her last. Once she stuck her head into a dumbwaiter to get some food for James, who had finally recovered enough from his war injuries to have an appetite, and I was certain the dumbwaiter was going to crash onto her head and kill her instantly. Another time, when she and Lord Bellamy went to fetch James from a hospital in France (and Hazel and Georgina had a fight over whether he should be moved), I was sure the ambulance would crash on the way back. Hazel lived on, though, show after show, until there came the thirteenth episode. As soon as they mentioned the plague, I knew that would be it. It was. The particular plague Hazel died of was the Spanish influenza, which, according to Alistair Cooke, was the last true pandemic. I was sorry that Alistair Cooke had so much more to say about the plague than he did about the death of Hazel, but perhaps he has become wary of commenting on the show itself after everyone (including me) took offense at some of the things he had to say about George Sand.

Of course, Hazel should never have married James Bellamy in the first place. James is a big baby. Hazel should have married Lord Bellamy, which was impossible since Lady Marjorie had just gone down on the *Titanic*. Or she should have run off with the upwardly mobile air ace, which was impossible since he was killed on the very next show after she met him, along with Rose's fiancé, Gregory. (I never laid eyes on Gregory, but Kenny tells me he was a very interesting man, a natural radical, who met Rose by sitting on her cake.) Hazel's finest moment was the show when she met the ace, and they went dancing, and she wore a dress with tiny, delicate beaded straps, and turned out to have the most beautiful back I have ever seen. But other than her back, and her fling with the ace, and her occasional success in telling Hudson off, and her premature death, Hazel left something to be desired. Not as far as Ann is concerned, but certainly as far as Martha is concerned. "Let's face it," said Martha. "Hazel was a pill." In fairness, we might all be pills if we had had to spend our lives sitting on a chesterfield couch pouring tea, but that's no excuse, I suppose. Hazel *was* a pill (though not nearly as terrible a pill as Abigail Adams and her entire family), and she really ought to have married an older man who wanted nothing more than to go to bed early. Still, James had no cause to treat her so badly. Kenny is the only person I know who has a kind word to say for James, and here it is: "Somewhere there must be something good about him that we'll find out about eventually." Actually, James did have a couple of good weeks there, when he returned from the front to report the army was dropping like flies, but I am told by a reliable source that his behavior was derivative of Siegfried Sassoon, and in any case, he shortly thereafter reverted to type. The worst James ever treated Hazel—aside from when she was sick and dying of the plague and he was playing rummy with his father's new fiancée, the Scottish widow—was when she had her miscarriage, and he totally ignored her, and went off dancing with Cousin Georgina.

Which brings us to Cousin Georgina. Martha doesn't much like Georgina either. This puzzles me. I can understand not liking Hazel and liking Georgina, or not liking Georgina and liking Hazel, but not liking both of them? Georgina was a true ninny when she arrived in the Bellamy household, and she hung around with Daisy, who is the most unrelenting ninny in television history. (For example, when Rose found out that Gregory had left her twelve hundred pounds, Daisy said: "Some people have all the luck." I rest my case.) But Georgina has become a wonderful nurse, and I'm proud of her. Also, her face is even more beautiful than Hazel's back. As for the burning question preoccupying us all—will Georgina marry James now that Hazel is dead?—I say no. (Martha says yes.) Georgina sees through James. I know it. I see her marrying the one-armed officer she went off to Paris with, if only because she is the only person on the show saintly enough to marry a man with one arm. Ann, on the other hand, does not trust Georgina as far as she can spit. "I know she was a great nurse," says Ann, "but she reminds me of those bitchy women you went to college with who were great biology students. She has no heart." There is indeed some recent evidence pointing to Georgina's heartlessness: when Hazel died, she went off to a party. But the war was over, and who could blame her? I was far more shocked at the la-di-da way Lord Bellamy behaved; he got off an Alistair Cooke-like remark about the plague itself, and that was that. Only Rose was magnificent about it. Ann thinks the reason everyone (except Rose) behaved so unemotionally about Hazel's death was that she was a petit bourgeois and they had never accepted her. I disagree. I think it's possible that the same person who tipped me off about Hazel's death tipped off the Bellamy household, and they just weren't all that surprised when it finally happened.

Even Martha loves Rose. Rose reminds me, in some metaphysical way, of Loretta Haggers. She is so good, so honest, so pure, so straight and so plucky. Kenny worries that Rose is going to leave the show now that she has come into all this money, but I say she'll never leave: the actress who plays Rose created the show itself, so she'll never be got rid of. I sometimes wonder how they do get rid of people at that show. They sank Lady Marjorie, I read somewhere, because the actress playing her wanted to take a vacation in Europe. But what about Hazel? Did they know all along? Did they hire her in the beginning and say, "Look here, Hazel, we'll carry you through World War One, but then you're through"? Or did they hire her planning to use her straight through the Depression? Did she do something to antagonize them? Did she know she was going to die, and if so, when?

We all know that Mrs. Bridges and Hudson are going to get married at the end of the next batch of episodes, which have already been shown in England. The reason we all know this is that the information was mentioned in the obituary of the actress who played Mrs. Bridges, who died of the flu in real life in Essex a couple of weeks before Hazel died of the flu on television in America. Was this planned too? Did they say to her, "Well, Mrs. Bridges, we'll give you a nice fat part for the entire series and marry you off to the butler in the end, but shortly thereafter you'll have to die"? I wonder. I also wonder how I'm going to feel about Mrs. Bridges and Hudson getting married. There's something a little too neat about it. Besides, Mrs. Bridges is a much better person than Hudson, who has become a mealy-mouthed hypocrite as well as a staunch defender of the British class system. All this would probably be all right and deliciously in character except that it is beginning to look as if Hudson is going to personify, in microcosm, the entire rise of Fascism in Europe. Ann is more concerned on this point than I am.

As for Edward and Daisy, they talk a lot about leaving the Bellamy household, but it is Kenny's theory that they are beginning to sound more and more like the three sisters and Moscow. Which is a shame, because I wish they would leave.

Here are some things we all agree on:

We are all terribly worried that Rose will never find a man.

We all miss Lady Marjorie a lot more than the Bellamys do, and are extremely apprehensive about meeting the Scottish widow's children.

We all think the best show of the year was the one with the scene in the train station with the dying and wounded soldiers. The second-best show was the one in which Gregory and the ace died.

We would all like to know some of the technical details of the show—how the writers are picked, how much of the plot is planned ahead of time—but it is too dangerous to find out. Someone, in the course of giving out the information, might let slip a crucial turn of the plot. We would all rather die than know what is going to happen.

Mostly, we all wish *Upstairs, Downstairs* would last forever.

July, 1976

PORTER
GOES
TO
THE
CONVENTION

PORTER checked into his hotel on Sunday night and went to Madison Square Garden to pick up his credentials. He wasn't sure what he was going to need them for, since his story had fallen through. Porter was a reporter for the *Tulark Morning Herald* of Tulark, Idaho, and his editor had sent him to the Democratic convention to cover the mayor of Tulark, J. Neal Dudley, who was a delegate. "Just follow him around," said the editor. Porter had had big plans. He would follow Dudley to the Empire State Building and the Statue of Liberty. He would follow him into a taxi and they would have a funny experience with a New York cabdriver. He would follow him to Eighth Avenue, where J. Neal Dudley would be mugged while Porter looked on helplessly, taking notes. He would follow him to dinner at Windows on the World, where with any luck Dudley would be thrown out for wearing a leisure suit.

Porter had begun by following Dudley to the Boise airport and onto the plane to New York. After a couple of drinks, he asked Dudley what he planned to do at the convention.

"Fuck my eyes out," said Dudley, "and if I catch you within twenty feet of my room I'll kill you."

"I'm supposed to follow you around," said Porter.

"Make it up," said J. Neal Dudley.

Dudley got into a cab at Kennedy airport and vanished. Porter got onto the bus and rode to his hotel. It occurred to him that if he could just find J. Neal Dudley fucking his eyes out, he could bring down the administration of Tulark, Idaho, such as it was.

On the other hand, Porter had read enough articles in journalism reviews to realize that he would have to find J. Neal Dudley in flagrante with a secretary who could not take shorthand and who had been flown into town on a ticket paid for with the proceeds from a secret sale of Tulark municipal bonds. Otherwise, his editor would refuse to print the story on the grounds that it was an invasion of J. Neal Dudley's privacy and a surefire way for the paper to lose the advertising from J. Neal Dudley's appliance dealership.

Porter decided to forget it. He would make the story up. He could always talk to enough delegates to put something together about what J. Neal Dudley would have done at the convention had he actually attended it.

So after getting his credentials, Porter set out to find a delegate. He went to the Statler Hilton lobby and spotted a large man wearing a ridiculous hat. Porter approached him.

"Porter of the *Tulark Morning Herald*," he said.

"Ken Franklin of *Newsday*," said the man in the hat. "Can I interview you?"

"I beg your pardon?" said Porter.

Franklin explained that he was the media reporter for *Newsday* and he just wanted to ask Porter the questions he'd been asking other reporters.

"Sure," said Porter. "Shoot."

"What are you planning to write about?" asked Franklin.

"I don't know," said Porter.

"That's what they all say," said Franklin. "There are twice as many media people here as delegates, and there's no story."

"There's no story?" said Porter.

"That's what they all say," said Franklin.

"What else do they all say?" said Porter.

"They all say that because there's no news story, there are no feature stories either."

"What about the hookers?" said Porter.

"All the hookers are taken," said Franklin. "The *New York Post* signed them all to exclusive contracts last week."

Porter bought himself a beer in the bar and looked around. He spotted a man wearing delegate's credentials and went over to him.

"Porter of the *Tulark Morning Herald*," he said.

"Suzanne Cox of the *Chicago Tribune*," said the woman sitting next to the delegate. "Get lost. This one's mine for the week."

"Could I ask *you* a question?" Porter said to Suzanne Cox.

"No, you can't," said a small boy next to Miss Cox.

"Who are you?" asked Porter.

"Brian Finley," said the boy. "I'm a reporter from *Children's Express*, and *I'm* covering *her*."

"Who's covering you?" asked Porter.

"Scotty Reston," said Brian Finley, "but he's gone to the men's room."

"I see," said Porter and went back to the bar.

"Jarvis of *Time* magazine," said a voice behind him. He turned around. Jarvis of *Time* magazine was very pretty. She was also a media reporter.

"Porter of the *Tulark Morning Herald*," Porter said. "I don't know what I'm writing about. There's no story. Because there's no news story, there are no feature stories either."

"What about the hookers?" said Jarvis.

"The hookers are taken," said Porter.

"Oh, God," said Jarvis. "I wonder if my writer knows that."

"Your writer?" said Porter, but Jarvis had rushed out of the bar.

Monday night Porter got a floor pass and watched Sally Quinn and Ben Bradlee being photographed. Then he joined a large crowd that was watching in disbelief as Evans and Novak had a conversation with each other. In the distance, Porter could hear Barbara Jordan speaking, but just barely. He wished he had stayed in his room and watched the convention on television. When the session ended, he bumped into Ken Franklin from *Newsday*.

"What are you writing about?" asked Franklin.

"I don't know," said Porter.

"Nobody's saying that today," said Franklin. "Today people have figured out what they're doing."

"Not me," said Porter.

Franklin took Porter to the *Rolling Stone* party that night. When they arrived, several hundred people on the street were pushing up against the door to the party, and several dozen police were trying to hold them back.

"Who's that with Seymour Hersh?" someone asked.

"Paul Newman," someone answered.

Porter managed to push his way up to the front door, but it was locked. Every so often, a man would appear at the door and point out someone in the crowd and the police would scoop up the someone and get him through the door. Porter squeezed in with Walter Cronkite's entourage, but once inside he found that the only topic of conversation was what was going on outside. A large group of people upstairs were watching a television monitor showing pictures of the scene on the street, and another large group of people were watching themselves on a public-access television channel.

"Porter of the *Tulark Morning Herald!*" a voice shouted.

Porter looked around. It was Jarvis of *Time* magazine.

"What are you doing?" she said.

"Leaving," he said. "Do you want to come?"

"Yes," said Jarvis.

Later, in Porter's hotel room, Jarvis began to undress. "I hope this is off the record," she said.

"Likewise," said Porter.

At that moment, the phone rang.

"Porter of the *Tulark Morning Herald*," said Porter.

"This is the New York City police," said a man on the phone. "We picked up a naked man dancing on Thirty-sixth Street. He says he's the mayor of Tulark, Idaho. Your name was in his pocket."

"Is he with his secretary?" asked Porter.

"Yes," said the policeman.

"Was she flown here on city money?" asked Porter.

"Yes," said the policeman.

"Can she take shorthand?"

"No," said the policeman.

"I'll be right there," said Porter. He put down the phone and started to dress. "I'm sorry, Jarvis," he said. "I have to go out to become a media star."

"That's all right," said Jarvis. "I can wait."

October, 1976

GOURMET
MAGAZINE

I'M not sure you can make a generalization on this basis, which is the basis of twice, but here goes: whenever I get married, I start buying *Gourmet* magazine. I think of it as my own personal bride's disease. The first time I started buying it was in 1967, when everyone my age in New York City spent hours talking about things like where to buy the best pistachio nuts. Someone recently told me that his marriage broke up during that period on account of veal Orloff, and I knew exactly what he meant. Hostesses were always making dinners that made you feel guilty, meals that took days to prepare and contained endless numbers of courses requiring endless numbers of plates resulting in an endless series of guests rising to help clear. Every time the conversation veered away from the food, the hostess looked hurt.

I got very involved in this stuff. Once I served a six-course Chinese dinner to twelve people, none of whom I still speak to, although not because of the dinner. I also specialized in little Greek appetizers that involved a great deal of playing with rice, and I once produced something known as the Brazilian national dish. Then, one night at a dinner party, a man I know looked up from his chocolate mousse and said, "Is this Julia's?" and I knew it was time to get off.

I can date that moment almost precisely—it was in December, 1972—because that's when I stopped buying *Gourmet* magazine the first time around. And I can date that last *Gourmet* precisely because I have never thrown out a copy of the magazine. At the end of each month, I place it on the top of the kitchen bookshelf, and there it lies, undisturbed, forever. I have never once looked at a copy of *Gourmet* after its month was up. But I keep them because you never know when you might need to. One of the tricky things about the recipes in *Gourmet* is that they often refer back to recipes in previous copies of the magazine: for example, once a year, usually in January, *Gourmet* prints the recipe for pâte brisée, and if you throw out your January issue, you're sunk for the year. All the tart recipes thereafter call for "one recipe pâte brisée (January, 1976)" and that's that. The same thing holds for chicken stock. I realize that I have begun to sound as if I actually use the recipes in *Gourmet*, so I must stop here and correct that impression. I don't. I also realize that I have begun to sound as if I actually read *Gourmet*, and I'd better correct that impression too. I don't actually read it. I sort of look at it in a fairly ritualistic manner.

The first thing I turn to in *Gourmet* is the centerfold. The centerfold of the magazine contains the *Gourmet* menu of the month, followed by four color pages of pictures, followed by the recipes. In December the menu is usually for Christmas dinner, in November for Thanksgiving, in July for the Fourth, and in April—when I bought my first *Gourmet* in four years owing to my marriage that month to a man with a Cuisinart Food Processor—for Easter. The rest of the year there are fall luncheons and spring breakfasts, and so forth. But the point is not the menus but the pictures. The first picture each month is of the table of the month, and it is laid with the china and crystal and silver of the month. That most of the manufacturers of this china and crystal and silver advertise in *Gourmet* should not concern us now; that comes later in the ritual. The table and all the things on it look remarkably similar every issue: very formal, slightly stuffy, and extremely elegant in a cut-glass, old-moneyed way. The three pages of pictures that follow are of the food, which looks just as stuffy and formal and elegant as the table itself. It would never occur to anyone at *Gourmet* to take the kind of sleek, witty food photographs I associate with the *Life* "Great Dinners" series, or the crammed, decadent pictures the women's magazines specialize in. *Gourmet* gives you a full-page color picture of an incredibly serious rack of lamb persillé sitting on a somber Blue Canton platter by Motta-hedeh Historic Charleston Reproductions sitting on a stiff eighteenth-century English mahogany table from Charles Deacon & Son—and it's no wonder I never cook anything from this magazine: the pictures are so reverent I almost feel I ought to pray to them.

After the centerfold I always turn to a section called "Sugar and Spice." This is the letters-to-the-editor department, and by all rights it should be called just plain "Sugar." I have never seen a letter in *Gourmet* that was remotely spicy, much less moderately critical. "I have culled so many fine recipes from your magazine that I feel it's time to do the sharing. . . ." "My husband and I have had many pleasant meals from recipes in *Gourmet* and we hope your readers will enjoy the following. . . ." Mrs. S. C. Rooney of Vancouver, B.C., writes to say that she and her husband leaf through *Gourmet* before every trip and would never have seen the Amalfi Drive but for the February, 1972, issue. "It is truly remarkable how you maintain such a high standard for every issue," she says. Almost every letter then goes on to present the writer's rec-ipe—brownies Weinstein, piquant mushrooms Potthoff, golden marinade Wyeth, Parmesan puff Jupenlaz. "Sirs," writes Margy Newman of Beverly Hills, "recently I found myself with two ripe bananas, an upcoming weekend out of town, and an hour until dinnertime. With one eye on my food processor and the other on some prunes, I proceeded to invent Prune Banana Whip Newman." The recipe for one prune banana whip Newman (April, 1976) followed.

"You Asked For It" comes next. This is the section where readers write in for recipes from restaurants they have fre-quented and *Gourmet* provides them. I look at this section for two reasons: first, on the chance that someone has written in for the recipe for the tarte Tatin at Maxwell's Plum in New York, which I would like to know how to make, and second, for the puns. "Here is the scoop du jour," goes the introduction to peach ice cream Jordan Pond House. "We'd be berry happy," *Gourmet* writes in the course of delivering a recipe for blueberry blintzes. "Rather than waffling about, here is a recipe for chocolate waffles." "To satisfy your yen for tempura, here is Hibachi's shrimp tempura." I could go on, but I won't; I do want to mention, though, that the person who writes these also seems to write the headlines on the "Sugar and Spice" column—at least I think I detect the same fine hand in such headlines as "Curry Favor," "The Berry Best" and "Something Fishy."

I skip the travel pieces, many of which are written by ladies with three names. "If Provence did not exist, the poets would be forced to invent it, for it is a lyrical landscape and to know it is to be its loving captive for life." Like that. Then I skip the restaurant reviews. *Gourmet* never prints unfavorable restaurant reviews; in fact, one of its critics is so determined not to find fault anywhere that he recently blamed himself for a bad dish he was served at the Soho Charcuterie: "The potatoes that came with it (savoyarde?—hard to tell) were disappointingly nondescript and cold, but I seemed to be having bad luck with potatoes *wherever* I went." Then I skip the special features on eggplant and dill and the like, because I have to get on to the ads.

Gourmet carries advertisements for a wide array of upper-class consumer goods (Rolls-Royce, De Beers diamonds, Galliano, etc.); the thing is to compare these ads to the editorial content of the magazine. I start by checking out the *Gourmet* holiday of the month—in May, 1976, for example, it was Helsinki—and then I count the number of ads in the magazine for things Finnish. Then I like to check the restaurants reviewed in the front against the restaurant ads in the back. Then, of course, I compare the china, silver and crystal in the menu of the month against the china, silver and crystal ads. All this is quite satisfying and turns out about the way you might suspect.

After that, I am pretty much through looking at *Gourmet* magazine. And where has it gotten me, you may ask. I've been trying to figure that out myself. Last April, when I began my second round, I think I expected that this time I would get around to cooking something from it. Then May passed and I failed to make the rhubarb tart pictured in the centerfold and I gave up in the recipe department. At that point, it occurred to me that perhaps I bought *Gourmet* because I figured it was the closest I would ever get to being a gentile. But that's not it either. The real reason, I'm afraid, has simply to do with food and life, particularly married life. "Does everyone who gets married talk about furniture?" my friend Bud Trillin once asked. No. Only for a while. After that you talk about pistachio nuts.

December, 1976

THE ONTARIO BULLETIN

TWO years ago, my husband bought a cooperative in the Ontario Apartments in Washington, D.C. The Ontario is an old building as Washington apartment buildings go, turn of the century, to be imprecise, and it has high ceilings, considerable woodwork, occasional marble and views of various capital sights. It also has the *Ontario Bulletin*. The *Ontario Bulletin* is a mimeographed newsletter that arrives every month or so in the mailbox. It is supplemented by numerous urgent memos and elevator notices; many of these concern crime. The Ontario is located in what is charitably called a marginal neighborhood, and all of us who live there look for signs that it is on the verge of becoming less marginal. The fact that the local movie theater is switching from Spanish-language films to English-language films is considered a good sign. The current memo in the elevator is not: "During the past eight weeks, FIVE ONTARIO WOMEN HAVE HAD THEIR PURSES SNATCHED on the grounds or close by. Three of these events occurred this week." This memo, written by Sue Lindgren, chairperson, Security Committee, goes on to state: "Fortunately, none of the victims was seriously injured and no building keys were lost." We were all relieved to read this, though I suspect that Christine Turpin was primarily relieved to read the part about the keys. Mrs. Turpin was president of the Ontario during the crime wave of May, 1976, when she wrote a particularly fine example of what I think of as the Turpin School of memo writing:

"There have been *three purse snatchings* at the Ontario's front door in the last *two weeks* causing *lock changes twice* in the same period. All three incidents occurred in daylight hours; the three 'victims'—all women—were returning from grocery stores on Columbia Road. Two of the three had ignored repeated and publicized advice: DO NOT CARRY BUILDING KEYS IN YOUR POCKETBOOKS. They also ignored other personal safety precautions. Much as we sympathize with them over their frightening experience and over the loss of their personal belongings, the fact remains that had these 'victims' heeded the warnings, everyone at the Ontario would have been spared the inconvenience of a second lock/key change in two weeks as well as the expenditure of $250 for replacements."

As far as I can tell, several of the early warnings Mrs. Turpin refers to appeared in the *Ontario Bulletin*, but I can hardly blame the "victims" for not noticing them. Until recently, the *Ontario Bulletin* was written by Mildred A. Pappas, who appears to be as blithe and good-humored as Mrs. Turpin is the opposite. Here and there Mrs. Pappas tucks in a late-breaking crime story: "As we were going to press Security Chairman Sue Lindgren called to say that the cigarette machine in the basement had been vandalized and that both cigarettes and some change were missing. There were no known suspects at the time of the call." But Mrs. Pappas has a firm editorial philosophy which she expressed in the January, 1975, *Bulletin:* "Both the trivial and the important are vital in portraying a clear picture of life in the Ontario—or anywhere else." And she has such a charming way with the trivial that her readers really ought to be forgiven their apparent tendency to skip over the important. In the February, 1975, *Bulletin,* for example, Mrs. Pappas does mention the business of not putting keys into pocketbooks, but that item pales next to the report on the revival of a limp African violet at the Houseplant Clinic, and it fades into insignificance next to the tantalizing mention of the removal of a hornets' nest from Elsie Carpenter's dining room window.

The information on the hornets' nest appeared in a regular feature of the *Bulletin* called "News and Notes," which includes birthdays, operations, recent houseguests and distinguished achievements of residents, as well as small bits of miscellaneous information like the announcement of the founding of the Ad Hoc Friends of the Pool Table Committee. Other regular sections of the publication are "The Travelers Return," a list of recent trips by residents; and "Committee Reports," summaries of the doings of the various building committees, of which there are nine. (This figure does not include the committee for the pool table, which has since disbanded, having successfully restored the table to use in the basement Green Room, which was recently and unaccountably painted yellow during the 1976 Painting Project.) The Ontario is surrounded by trees and gardens, so the *Bulletin* often mentions the planting of a new azalea or juniper tree, and it recently devoted an entire page to the final chapter of the eight-year controversy of the Great Red Oak, cut down on August 27, 1976, after the board of directors overruled what was known as the "wait and see" policy of the High Tree Subcommittee. Articles like these are often illustrated with simple drawings of birds and leaves. Occasionally, a photograph is used, but only on a major story like the flap over the water bill.

Ontario residents first learned of the water-bill flap in a July, 1975, *Bulletin* article headlined A SHOCKING BILL FOR A SHOCKING WASTE: "Chairman Chris Turpin has just announced that a staggering (and unbudgeted) $1,660.94 water bill for the last quarter has just been received, adding that the amount is more than *three* times the amount for the preceding quarter. A wrong billing? No. Uncommon usage for bad water, etc.? No. . . . The water company has advanced the opinion that only one malfunctioning toilet allowed to run continuously can be the cause. . . . The chairman stated that the board will decide on a method of payment of the unprecedented bill at its July meeting, the alternatives being (1) to find the resident or residents responsible and to bill accordingly, or (2) to specially assess *all* residents (owners and tenants alike) approximately $10 each to settle the bill."

For a month, we anxiously awaited word of what was up. Would ten dollars be added to the maintenance? Or would Chairman Turpin lead the Ad Hoc Committee on the Unprecedented Water Bill through each apartment in search of the hypothetical malfunctioning toilet? Finally, the July *Bulletin* appeared, with a terse report suggesting that the investigation was closing in: the prime suspect turned out to be not some irresponsible resident but the building's thirty-five-year-old water meter, which had just been removed for inspection by the water company. Meanwhile, Clarence K. Streit, a resident who was apparently unaware that human error was about to be ruled out, made a guest appearance in the *Bulletin* as the author of the Flask Water Dollar Saver. "It is quite practical," he wrote, "to save three pints of water every time one flushes a toilet. We have been doing it for a couple of years." According to Streit, if everyone in the building placed three pint flasks in his toilet tank, then Ontario could save 150,000 gallons of water a year—or, as he put it, *150,000* gallons of water a year. Mrs. Pappas urged residents who took up Streit's suggestion to submit their names for publication in order to encourage others. No one did; at least I assume no one did from the fact that Mrs. Pappas never again referred to the Flask Water Dollar Saver Plan. In the August *Bulletin*, however, the water meter was definitely fingered; it turned out to be not just out of order but thoroughly obsolete. A photograph of the new water meter appeared as an illustration.

If I have any complaint at all about the *Ontario Bulletin*, it is simply that its even-handed approach occasionally leaves something to be desired. Accurate reporting was simply not enough to convey the passions engendered by the paint selections of the 1976 Painting Project, nor was it adequate to describe the diabolical maneuverings of President Turpin and the Ontario board in the face of these passions. Residents who read the loving tribute in the August *Bulletin* to the Great Red Oak and the account of its mysterious incurable disease could hardly have been prepared for the stunning moment at the annual meeting in September when it was moved that no tree be cut down without a membership vote. Mrs. Pappas's low-key description of the restored iron grille entrance doors—"Unfortunately, the 'Ontario' inscription now faces the interior of the building since it could not be relocated from its solid iron casting to the outside"—does not quite do justice to the situation.

And I cannot imagine that *Bulletin* readers were in any position to judge the item in March, 1976, which announced Dr. Allan Angerio's resignation as House Maintenance Committee Chairman. "In protest of the Board's sanction of extensive remodeling in a neighboring apartment, Dr. Allan

Angerio has resigned five months after his appointment. In a recently circulated letter to all residents Dr. Angerio states that during the extended period of renovation he was 'unable to use my apartment for either business or pleasure.' He also states that his letter has engendered a considerable response from the membership, many of whom have indicated interest in a proposed revision of the Bylaws and House Rules of the Corporation to preclude further extensive structural 'modernization' efforts in the Ontario." This is certainly a fair summary of what happened—but it is not enough. I know. I am married to the man who hired the contractor who accidentally drilled the hole into Dr. Angerio's bedroom wall.

In any case, mine are small complaints. The main function of a newspaper is to let its readers know what's going on; I doubt that there are many communities that are served as well by their local newspapers as this tiny community is by the *Ontario Bulletin*. And I would feel even more warmly toward the publication than I do but for the fear I have, each month, that I will pick it up to read: "The residents of 605 had a fight last Thursday night over the fact that one person in the apartment never closes her closet doors." I like neighborhoods, you see, but I worry about neighbors. Fortunately, my husband and I also have an apartment in New York. And I was extremely pleased several weeks ago when we moved to new quarters there in an extremely unfriendly-looking brownstone on an extremely haughty block. In the course of the week's move, we carried some garbage out of the apartment and left it on the street for the garbage collectors. Ten minutes later—*ten minutes later*—a memo arrived from the 74th Street Block Association concerning the block rules on refuse. I'm not going to quote from it. All I want to say is that its author, Emma Preziosi, while not in the same league with Christine Turpin, definitely shows promise.

March, 1977

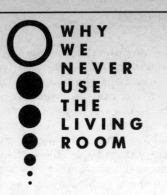

WHY WE NEVER USE THE LIVING ROOM

HAVE a nice living room. You should come sit in it some day. You will undoubtedly be alone when you do, however, because no one ever sits in the living room. (Unless we have company. Then we sit in the living room. Otherwise, never.) We talk a lot about the fact that no one ever sits in the living room. It makes us all sad. The living room is the prettiest room in the apartment. It has a fireplace and moldings. It has a slice of a view of the river. It is a cheerful room furnished in light colors. The couches in it were recently cleaned by men with small machines. It always looks neat and tidy. That's because no one ever uses it, I know that, but still. You should see it. I already said that, but I mean it.

Many reasons have been put forward for why we never use the living room. Last year I came to believe that the main reason was the lamps. So I got new lamps. They are much more attractive than the old lamps. Also they make the room much brighter. It is now possible to see in the living room. It is even possible to read in the living room. Still, we don't use the living room. Sometimes, in the evening, when we are feeling particularly melancholy about not using the living room, we wander into it and admire the new lamps and talk about what I have this year come to believe are the reasons for its enduring emptiness. Perhaps if there were a phone in the living room, but I don't like phones in living rooms. Perhaps if there were a television set, but I feel as strongly about television sets in living rooms as I do about phones. Perhaps new window treatments would help, but talk of window treatments makes me even more melancholy than the plight of the living room.

Years ago, when I lived in a two-room apartment, I never used the living room either. I used the bedroom. I worked in the bedroom, I ate in the bedroom, I slept in the bedroom. Now I have an apartment with many rooms. I work in the study, I eat in the kitchen, I continue to sleep in the bedroom. Sometimes I think about moving the bed into the living room. This would not solve the problem of why we never use the living room—because the living room would then be the bedroom—but at least we would use the room that is supposed to be the living room for something. The trouble with the idea is that the living room has no closets and is a long way from the bathroom. Also, I am too old to have a bed in the living room.

Every time I walk from the bedroom or the study to the kitchen I pass the living room and take a long, fond look at it. It's a lovely room. It might as well be one of those rooms in Bloomingdale's with a velvet rope cordoned across it for all the good it does me.

When I was growing up, I had a friend named Lillian who had no living room furniture. She lived in a large house in Beverly Hills, and the living room was empty. I always wondered why. I always supposed it was because her mother was having trouble deciding on a color scheme. Color schemes were important in those days. I had a friend named Arlene whose house was famous for having a color scheme in every room, including the breakfast nook, which was charcoal gray and pink. Anyway, a few years ago, Lillian was in New York and I finally got up the nerve to ask her why her family had never had any living room furniture. She told me that her father had given her mother a choice of living room furniture or a pool, and her mother had chosen the pool. I salute my friend Lillian's mother. She obviously understood something that I am still having trouble absorbing, which is this: at least you can swim in a pool.

But what can you do in a living room? Tell me. I really want to know. I know what to do in a charcoal gray and pink breakfast nook, but the only thing I can think of to do in a living room is living, and I clearly don't have a clue as to what that consists of, especially if you rule out eating, sleeping, working and swimming. I'm sure that some people are good at it, whatever it is. They probably lie around in a marginally useful way. They probably contemplate life. They probably have servants and drinks before dinner and coffee table books. They probably think of themselves as civilized.

My living room sits in my apartment, a silent snobbish presence, secretly contemptuous that I don't know what to do with a room that has no clear function. I'm sure it wishes I were more civilized; I'm positive it hopes that someday I will grow up and spend a little time in it. And some day I will. Some day when I am very old. By that time I will be no good at all at eating, sleeping, working and swimming, but I won't mind, because I will finally have found a use for the living room. It is obviously the perfect place in which to die.

December, 1985

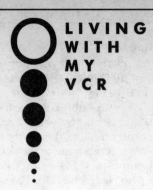

LIVING WITH MY VCR

WHEN all this started, two years ago, I did not have a video cassette recorder. What I had was a position on video cassette recorders. I was against them. It seemed to me that the fundamental idea of VCRs—which is that if you go out and miss what's on television, you can always watch it later— flew in the face of almost the only thing I truly believed— which is that the whole point of going out is to miss what's on television. Let's face it: part of being a grownup is that every day you have to choose between going out at night or staying home, and it is one of life's unhappy truths that there is not enough time to do both.

Finally, though, I broke down, but not entirely. I did not buy a video cassette recorder. I rented one. And I didn't rent one for myself—I myself intended to stand firm and hold to my only principle. I rented one for my children. For $29 a month, I would tape *The Wizard of Oz* and *Mary Poppins* and *Born Free*, and my children would be able to watch them from time to time. In six months, when my rental contract expired, I would re-evaluate.

For quite a while, I taped for my children. Of course I had to subscribe to Home Box Office and Cinemax in addition to my normal cable service, for $19 more a month—

but for the children. I taped *Oliver* and *Annie* and *My Fair Lady* for the children. And then I stopped taping for the children—who don't watch much television, in any case— and started to tape for myself.

I now tape for myself all the time. I tape when I am out, I tape when I am at home and doing other things, and I tape when I am asleep. At this very moment as I am typing, I am taping. The entire length of my bedroom bookshelf has been turned over to video cassettes, mostly of movies, they are numbered and indexed and stacked in order in a household where absolutely nothing else is. Occasionally I find myself browsing through publications like *Video Review* and worrying whether I shouldn't switch to basechrome videotape or have my heads cleaned or upgrade to a machine that does six or seven things at once and can be set to tape six or seven months in advance. No doubt I will soon find myself shopping at some video village for special racks and storage systems especially made for what is known as "the serious collector."

How this happened, how I became a compulsive video-taper, is a mystery to me, because my position on video cassette recorders is very much the same as the one I started with. I am still against them. Now, though, I am against them for different reasons: now I hate them out of knowl-edge rather than ignorance. The other technological break-throughs that have made their way into my life after my initial pigheaded opposition to them—like the electric type-writer and the Cuisinart—have all settled peacefully into my household. I never think about them except when I'm using them, and when I'm using them I take them for granted. They do exactly what I want them to do. I put the slicing disc into the Cuisinart, and damned if the thing doesn't slice things up just the way it's supposed to. But there's no taking a VCR for granted. It squats there, next to the television, ready to rebuke any fool who expects something of it.

A child can operate a VCR, of course. Only a few ma-neuvers are required to tape something, and only a few more are required to tape something while you are out. You must set the timer to the correct time you wish the recording to begin and end. You must punch the channel selector. You must insert a videotape. And you must switch the On button to Time Record. Theoretically, you can then go out and have a high old time, knowing that even if you waste the evening, your video cassette recorder will not.

Sometimes things work out. Sometimes I return home, rewind the tape, and discover that the machine has recorded exactly what I'd hoped it would. But more often than not, what is on the tape is not at all what I'd intended; in fact, the moments leading up to the revelation of what is actually on my video cassettes are without doubt the most suspenseful of my humdrum existence. As I rewind the tape, I have no idea of what, if anything, will be on it; as I press the Play button, I have not a clue as to what in particular has gone wrong. All I ever know for certain is that something has.

Usually it's my fault. I admit it. I have misset the timer or channel selector or misread the newspaper listing. I have knelt at the feet of my machine and methodically, carefully, painstakingly set it—and set it wrong. This is extremely upsetting to me—I am normally quite competent when it comes to machines—but I can live with it. What is far more disturbing are the times when what has gone wrong is not my fault at all but the fault of outside forces over which I have no control whatsoever. The program listing in the newspaper lists the channel incorrectly. The cable guide inaccurately lists the length of the movie, lopping off the last ten minutes. The evening's schedule of television programming is thrown off by an athletic event. The educational station is having a fundraiser. You would be amazed at how often outside forces affect a video cassette recorder, and I think I am safe in saying that video cassette recorders are the only household appliances that outside forces are even relevant to. As a result, my video cassette library is a raggedy collection of near misses: *The Thin Man* without the opening; *King Kong* without the ending; a football game instead of *Murder She Wrote*; dozens of Channel 13 auctions and fundraisers instead of dozens of episodes of *Masterpiece Theatre*. All told, my success rate at videotaping is even lower than my success rate at buying clothes I turn out to like as much as I did in the store; the machine provides more opportunities per week to make mistakes than anything else in my life.

Every six months, I re-evaluate my rental contract. I have three options: I can buy the video cassette recorder, which I would never do because I hate it so much; I can cancel the contract and turn in the machine, which I would never do because I am so addicted to videotaping; or I can go on renting. I go on renting. In two years I have spent enough money renting to buy two video cassette recorders at the discount electronics place in the neighborhood, but I don't care. Renting is my way of deluding myself that I have some power over my VCR; it's my way of believing that I can still some day reject the machine in an ultimate way (by sending it back)—or else forgive it (by buying it)—for all the times it has rejected me.

In the meantime, I have my pathetic but ever-expanding collection of cassettes. "Why don't you just rent the movies?" a friend said to me recently, after I finished complaining about the fact that my *Maltese Falcon* now has a segment of *The Little House on the Prairie* in the middle of it. Rent them? What a bizarre suggestion. Then I would have to watch them. And I don't watch my videotapes. I don't have time. I would virtually have to watch my videotapes for the next two years just to catch up with what my VCR has recorded so far; and in any event, even if I did have time, the VCR would be taping and would therefore be unavailable for use in viewing. So I merely accumulate video cassettes. I haven't accumulated anything this mindlessly since my days in college, when I was obsessed with filling my bookshelf, it didn't matter with what; what mattered was that I believed that if I had a lot of books, it would say something about my intelligence and taste. On some level, I suppose I believe that if I have a lot of video cassettes, it will say something—not about my intelligence or taste, but about my intentions. I intend to live long enough to have time to watch my videotapes. Any way you look at it, that means forever.

December, 1984

WHEN HARRY MET SALLY DOT DOT DOT

THIS screenplay has my name on it, but it was very much a
collaboration, and before I write a word about the movie
itself, I want to write about how it got started. It began in
October 1984, when I got a call from my agent that Rob
Reiner and his producing partner Andrew Scheinman
wanted to have lunch to discuss a project. So we had a lunch,
and they told me about an idea they had for a movie about
a lawyer. I've forgotten the details. The point is, it didn't
interest me at all, and I couldn't imagine why they'd thought
of me in connection with it. I remember being slightly per-
plexed about whether to say straight off that the idea didn't
interest me or whether to play along for an hour so as not
to have that horrible awkwardness that can happen when
the meeting is over but the lunch must go on. I decided on
the former; and we then spent the rest of the lunch talking
about ourselves. Well, that isn't entirely true: we spent the
rest of the lunch talking about Rob and Andy. Rob was
divorced, and Andy was a bachelor—and they were both
extremely funny and candid about their lives as single men
in Los Angeles. When the lunch ended, we still didn't have
an idea for a movie; but we decided to meet again the next
time they were in New York.

And so, a month later, we got together. And threw around some more ideas, none of which I remember. But finally, Rob said he had an idea—he wanted to make a movie about a man and a woman who become friends, as opposed to lovers; they make a deliberate decision not to have sex because sex ruins everything; and then they have sex and it ruins everything. And I said, let's do it.

So we made a deal, and in February, Andy and Rob came back to New York and we sat around for several days and they told me some things. Appalling things. They told me, for instance, that when they finished having sex, they wanted to get up out of bed and go home. (Which became: HARRY: "How long do I have to lie here and hold her before I can get up and go home? Is thirty seconds enough? . . . How long do you like to be held afterwards? All night, right? . . . Somewhere between thirty seconds and all night is your problem." SALLY: "I don't have a problem.") They told me about the endless series of excuses they had concocted in order to make a middle-of-the-night getaway. (SALLY: "You know, I am so glad I never got involved with you. I just would have ended up being some woman you had to get up out of bed and leave at three o'clock in the morning and go clean your andirons. And you don't even have a fireplace. Not that I would know this.") They also told me that the reason they thought men and women couldn't be friends was that a man always wanted to sleep with a woman. Any woman. (HARRY: "No man can be friends with a woman he finds attractive. He always wants to have sex with her." SALLY: "So you're saying a man *can* be friends with a woman he finds unattractive." HARRY: "No. You pretty much want to nail them, too.") I say that these things were appalling, but the truth is that they weren't really a surprise; they were sort of my wildest nightmares of what men thought.

Rob and Andy and I noodled for hours over the questions raised by friendship, and sex, and life in general; and as we did, I realized—long before I had any idea of what was actually going to happen in the movie itself—that I had found a wonderful character in Rob Reiner. Rob is a very strange person. He is extremely funny, but he is also extremely depressed—or at least he was at the time; he talked constantly about how depressed he was. "You know how women have a base of makeup," he said to me. "I have a base of depression. Sometimes I sink below it. Sometimes I rise above it." This line went right into the first draft of the movie, but somewhere along the line Rob cut it. A mistake, I think, but never mind. Here's another from Rob on his depression: "I think I'm not ready for a relationship. When you're as depressed as I am . . . If the depression was lifted, I would be able to be with someone on my level. But it's like playing tennis on a windy day with someone who's worse than you are. They can do all right against you, they can win a couple of games, but there's too much wind. You know what I mean?" I have no idea what Rob was talking about, but as I wrote those words in my notebook I knew that I would use the lines somehow. And I did, and they were cut, and it was a mistake, and never mind.

The point is that Rob was depressed; but he wasn't at all depressed about being depressed; in fact, he loved his depression. And so does Harry. Harry honestly believes that he is a better person than Sally because he has what Sally generously calls a dark side. "Suppose nothing happens to you," he says in the first sequence of the movie. "Suppose you live there [New York] your whole life and nothing happens. You never meet anyone, you never become anything, and finally you die one of those New York deaths where nobody notices for two weeks until the smell drifts out into the hallway." Harry is genuinely proud to have thought of that possibility and to lay it at the feet of this shallow young woman he is stuck in a car with for eighteen hours. He is thrilled to be the prince of darkness, the master of the worst-case scenario, the man who is happy to tell you, as you find yourself in the beginning of a love affair, that what follows lust, inevitably, is post-lust: "You take someone to the airport, it's clearly the beginning of a relationship. That's why I've never taken anyone to the airport at the beginning of a relationship. . . . Because eventually things move on and you don't take someone to the airport, and I never wanted anyone to say to me, 'How come you never take me to the airport anymore?'"

So I began with a Harry, based on Rob. And because Harry was bleak and depressed, it followed absolutely that Sally would be cheerful and chirpy and relentlessly, pointlessly, unrealistically, idiotically optimistic. Which is, it turns out, very much like me. I'm not precisely chirpy, but I am the sort of person who is fine, I'm just fine, everything's fine. "I am over him," Sally says, when she isn't over him at all; I have uttered that line far too many times in my life, and far too many times I've made the mistake of believing it was true. Sally loves control—and I'm sorry to say that I do too. And inevitably, Sally's need to control her environment is connected to food. I say inevitably because food has always been something I write about—in part because it's the only thing I'm an expert on. But it wasn't my idea to use the way I order food as a character trait for Sally; well along in the process—third or fourth draft or so—Rob and Andy and I were ordering lunch for the fifth day in a row, and for the fifth day in a row my lunch order—for an avocado and bacon sandwich—consisted of an endless series of parenthetical remarks. I wanted the mayonnaise on the side. I wanted the bread toasted and slightly burnt. I wanted the bacon crisp. "I just like it the way I like it," I said, defensively, when the pattern was pointed out to me—and the line went into the script.

But all that came much later. In the beginning, I was more or less alone—with a male character based somewhat on Rob, and a female character based somewhat on me. And a subject. Which was not, by the way, whether men and women could be friends. The movie instead was a way for me to write about being single—about the difficult, frustrating, awful, funny search for happiness in an American city where the primary emotion is unrequited love. This is from my notes, February 5, 1985, Rob speaking: "This is a talk piece. There are no chase scenes. No food fights. This is walks, apartments, phones, restaurants, movies." Also from my notes, Rob again: "We're talking about a movie about two people who get each other from the breakup of the first big relationship in their lives to the beginning of the second. Transitional on some level. Who are friends, who don't have sex, who nurse each other and comfort each other and talk to each other and then finally do it and it's a mistake and recover from it and move into second relationships." Here's a scene from the first draft; it bit the dust early, too self-conscious, but I toss it in partly because I can't stand to waste anything, and partly because it perfectly sums up the movie I was trying to write:

SALLY: I think we should write a movie about our relationship.

HARRY: What's the plot?

SALLY: There are only two plots. The first is, an appealing character strives against great odds to achieve a worthwhile goal, and the second is, the bluebird of happiness is right in your own backyard. We're the first.

HARRY: An appealing character—

SALLY: *Two* appealing characters strive against great odds to achieve a worthwhile goal. Two people become friends at the end of the first major relationship of their lives and get each other to the next major relationship of their lives.

HARRY: I don't know anything about writing movies.

SALLY: Neither do I.

HARRY: But on the face of it—I don't want to be negative about it—

SALLY: Sure you do. You love being negative, it's who you are, embrace it—

HARRY: —but it seems to me that movies are supposed to be visual. We don't do anything visual. We just sit in restaurants and talk, or we sit on the phone and talk, or we sit in your apartment or my apartment and talk.

SALLY: In French movies they just talk.

HARRY: Do you speak French?

SALLY: Not really.

HARRY: What happens to the friends when each of them gets to the next major relationship of their lives?

SALLY: They're still going to be friends. They're going to be friends forever.

HARRY: I don't know, Sally. You know what happens. You meet somebody new and you take them to meet your friend, and you want them to like each other as much as you do, but they never do, they always see the friend as a threat to your relationship, and you try to stay just as good friends with your friend but eventually you don't really need each other as much because you've got a new friend, you've got someone you can talk to *and* fuck—

SALLY: Forget I mentioned it, okay?

They smile at each other.

HARRY: I love you. You know that.

SALLY: I love you too.

HARRY: When I say, "I love you," you know what I mean—

SALLY: I know what you mean. I know.

When Harry Met Sally started shooting in August 1988, almost four years after my first meeting with Rob and Andy. In the meantime I wrote a first draft about two people who get each other from the breakup of the first big relationship in their lives to the beginning of the second. Rob went off and made *Stand By Me*. We met again and decided that Harry and Sally belonged together. I wrote a second draft. Rob went off and made *The Princess Bride*. And then we all went to work together on the next (at least) five drafts of the movie. What had been called *Just Friends* and then *Play Melancholy Baby* went on to be called *Boy Meets Girl*; *Words of Love*; *It Had to Be You*; and *Harry, This Is Sally*. To name just a few of the titles. Mostly we called it "Untitled Rob Reiner Project." Rob suggested that we try inserting some older couples talking about how they met. *How They Met* was another title we considered for at least a day. And gradually, the script began to change, from something that was mostly mine, to something else.

Here is what I always say about screenwriting. When you write a script, it's like delivering a great big beautiful plain pizza, the one with only cheese and tomatoes. And then you give it to the director, and the director says, "I love this pizza. I am willing to commit to this pizza. But I really think this pizza should have mushrooms on it." And you say, "Mushrooms! Of course! I meant to put mushrooms on the pizza! Why didn't I think of that? Let's put some on immediately." And then someone else comes along and says, "I love this pizza too, but it really needs green peppers." "Great," you say. "Green peppers. Just the thing." And then someone else says, "Anchovies." There's always a fight over the anchovies. And when you get done, what you have is a pizza with everything. Sometimes it's wonderful. And sometimes you look at it and you think, I knew we shouldn't have put the green peppers onto it. Why didn't I say so at the time? Why didn't I lie down in traffic to prevent anyone's putting green peppers onto the pizza?

All this is a long way of saying that movies generally start out belonging to the writer and end up belonging to the director. If you're very lucky as a writer, you look at the director's movie and feel that it's your movie, too. As Rob and Andy and I worked on the movie, it changed: it became less quirky and much funnier; it became less mine and more theirs. But what made it possible for me to live through this process—which is actually called "The Process," a polite expression for the period when the writer, generally, gets screwed—was that Rob and I each had a character we owned. On most movies, what normally happens in the course of The Process is that the writer says one thing and the director says another thing, and in the end the most the writer can hope for is a compromise; what made this movie different was that Rob had a character who could say whatever he believed, and if I disagreed, I had Sally to say so for me.

And much as I would like to take full credit for what Sally says in the movie, the fact is that many of her best moments went into the script after the three of us began work on it together. "We told you about men," Rob and Andy said to me one day. "Now tell us about women." So I said, "Well, we could do something about sex fantasies." And I wrote the scene about Sally's sex fantasy. "What else?" they said. "Well," I said, "women send flowers to themselves in order to fool their boyfriends into thinking they have other suitors." And I wrote the scene about Marie sending flowers to herself. "What else?" Rob and Andy said. "Well," I said, "women fake orgasms." "Really?" they said. "Yes," I said. There was a long pause. I think I am correct in remembering the long pause. "All women?" they said. "Most women," I said. "At one time or another."

A few days later, Rob called. He and Andy had written a sequence about faking orgasms and they wanted to insert it at the end of the scene that was known (up to that time) as the andirons scene. He read it over the phone. I loved it. It went into the script. A few weeks later, we had our first actors' reading, and Meg Ryan, who by then was our Sally, suggested that Sally actually fake an orgasm in the delicatessen at the end of the scene. We loved it. It went into the script. And then Billy Crystal, our Harry, provided the funniest of the dozens of funny lines he brought with him to the movie; he suggested that a woman customer turn to a waiter, when Sally's orgasm was over, and say: "I'll have what she's having." The line, by the way, was delivered in the movie by Estelle Reiner, Rob's mother. So there you have it—a perfect example of how The Process works on the occasions when it works.

I don't want to sound Pollyannaish about any of this. Rob and I disagreed. We disagreed all the time. Rob believes that men and women can't be friends (HARRY: "Men and women can't be friends, because the sex part always gets in the way"). I disagree (SALLY: "That's not true. I have plenty of men friends and there's no sex involved"). And both of us are right. Which brings me to what *When Harry Met Sally* is really about—not, as I said, whether men and women can be friends, but about how different men and women are. The truth is that men don't want to be friends with women. Men know they don't understand women, and they don't much care. They want women as lovers, as wives, as mothers, but they're not really interested in them as friends. They have friends. Men are their friends. And they talk to their male friends about sports, and I have no idea what else.

Women, on the other hand, are dying to be friends with men. Women know they don't understand men, and it bothers them: they think that if only they could be friends with them, they would understand them and, what's more (and this is their gravest mistake), it would help. Women think if they could just understand men, they could *do something*. Women are always trying to *do something*. There are entire industries based on this premise, the most obvious one being the women's magazines—there are hundreds of them, there are probably five of them in darkest Zaire alone—that are based completely on the notion that women can *do something* where men are concerned: cook a perfect steak, or wear a perfect skirt, or dab a little perfume behind the knee. "Rub your thighs together when you walk," someone once wrote in *Cosmopolitan* magazine. "The squish-squish sound of nylon has a frenzying effect."

When a movie like *When Harry Met Sally* opens, people come to ask you questions about it. And for a few brief weeks, you become an expert. You seem quite wise. You give the impression that you knew what you were doing all along. You become an expert on friends, on the possibilities of love, on the differences between men and women. But the truth is that when you work on a movie, you don't sit around thinking, we're making a movie about the difference between men and women. Or whatever. You just do it. You say, this scene works for me, but this one doesn't. You say, this is good, but this could be funnier. You say, it's a little slow here, what could we do to speed it up? You say, this scene is long, and this scene isn't story, and we need a better button on this one.

And then they go off and shoot the movie and cut the movie and sometimes you get a movie that you're happy with. It's my experience that this happens very rarely. Once in a blue moon. *Blue Moon* was another title we considered for a minute or two. I mention it now so you will understand that even when you have a movie you're happy with, there's always something—in this case, the title—that you wish you could fix. But never mind.

1990

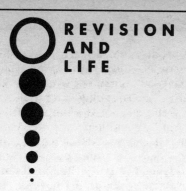

REVISION
AND
LIFE

I

HAVE been asked to write something for a textbook that is meant to teach college students something about writing and revision. I am happy to do this because I believe in revision. I have also been asked to save the early drafts of whatever I write, presumably to show these students the actual process of revision. This too I am happy to do. On the other hand, I suspect that there is just so much you can teach college students about revision; a gift for revision may be a developmental stage—like a 2-year-old's sudden ability to place one block on top of another—that comes along somewhat later, in one's mid–20's, say; most people may not be particularly good at it, or even interested in it, until then.

When I was in college, I revised nothing. I wrote out my papers in longhand, typed them up and turned them in. It would never have crossed my mind that what I had produced was only a first draft and that I had more work to do; the idea was to get to the end, and once you had got to the end you were finished. The same thinking, I might add, applied in life: I went pell-mell through my four years in college without a thought about whether I ought to do anything differently; the idea was to get to the end—to get out of school and become a journalist.

Which I became, in fairly short order. I learned as a journalist to revise on deadline. I learned to write an article a paragraph at a time—and to turn it in a paragraph at a time—and I arrived at the kind of writing and revising I do, which is basically a kind of typing and retyping. I am a great believer in this technique for the simple reason that I type faster than the wind. What I generally do is to start an article and get as far as I can—sometimes no farther in than a sentence or two—before running out of steam, ripping the piece of paper from the typewriter and starting all over again. I type over and over until I have got the beginning of the piece to the point where I am happy with it. I then am ready to plunge into the body of the article itself. This plunge usually requires something known as a transition. I approach a transition by completely retyping the opening of the article leading up to it in the hope that the ferocious speed of my typing will somehow catapult me into the next section of the piece. This does not work—what in fact catapults me into the next section is a concrete thought about what the next section ought to be about—but until I have the thought the typing keeps me busy, and keeps me from feeling something known as blocked.

Typing and retyping as if you know where you're going is a version of what therapists tell you to do when they suggest that you try changing from the outside in—that if you can't master the total commitment to whatever change you want to make, you can at least do all the extraneous things connected with it, which make it that much easier to get there. I was 25 years old the first time a therapist suggested that I try changing from the outside in. In those days, I used to spend quite a lot of time lying awake at night wondering what I should have said earlier in the evening and revising my lines. I mention this not just because it's a way of illustrating that a gift for revision is practically instinctive, but also (once again) because it's possible that a genuine ability at it doesn't really come into play until one is older—or at least older than 25, when it seemed to me that all that was required in my life and my work was the chance to change a few lines.

In my 30's, I began to write essays, one a month for *Esquire* magazine, and I am not exaggerating when I say that in the course of writing a short essay—1,500 words, that's only six double-spaced typewritten pages—I often used 300 or 400 pieces of typing paper, so often did I type and retype and catapult and recatapult myself, sometimes on each retyping moving not even a sentence farther from the spot I had reached the last time through. At the same time, though, I was polishing what I had already written: as I struggled with the middle of the article, I kept putting the beginning through the typewriter; as I approached the ending, the middle got its turn. (This is a kind of polishing that the word processor all but eliminates, which is why I don't use one. Word processors make it possible for a writer to change the sentences that clearly need changing without having to re-type the rest, but I believe that you can't always tell whether a sentence needs work until it rises up in revolt against your fingers as you retype it.) By the time I had produced what you might call a first draft—an entire article with a begin-ning, middle and end—the beginning was in more like 45th draft, the middle in 20th, and the end was almost newborn. For this reason, the beginnings of my essays are considerably better written than the ends, although I like to think no one ever notices this but me.

As I learned the essay form, writing became harder for me. I was finding a personal style, a voice if you will, a way of writing that looked chatty and informal. That wasn't the hard part—the hard part was that having found a voice, I had to work hard month to month not to seem as if I were repeating myself. At this point in this essay it will not surprise you to learn that the same sort of thing was operating in my life. I don't mean that my life had become harder—but that it was becoming clear that I had many more choices than had occurred to me when I was marching through my 20's. I no longer lost sleep over what I should have said. Not that I didn't care—it was just that I had moved to a new plane of late-night anxiety: I now wondered what I should have done. Whole areas of possible revision opened before me. What should I have done instead? What could I have done? What if I hadn't done it the way I did? What if I had a chance to do it over? What if I had a chance to do it over as a different person? These were the sorts of questions that kept me awake and led me into fiction, which at the very least (the level at which I practice it) is a chance to rework the events of your life so that you give the illusion of being the intelligence at the center of it, simultaneously managing to slip in all the lines that occurred to you later. Fiction, I suppose, is the ultimate shot at revision.

Now I am in my 40's and I write screenplays. Screenplays—if they are made into movies—are essentially collaborations, and movies are not a writer's medium, we all know this, and I don't want to dwell on the craft of screenwriting except insofar as it relates to revision. Because the moment you stop work on a script seems to be determined not by whether you think the draft is good but simply by whether shooting is about to begin: if it is, you get to call your script a final draft; and if it's not, you can always write another revision. This might seem to be a hateful way to live, but the odd thing is that it's somehow comforting; as long as you're revising, the project isn't dead. And by the same token, neither are you.

It was, as it happens, while thinking about all this one recent sleepless night that I figured out how to write this particular essay. I say "recent" in order to give a sense of immediacy and energy to the preceding sentence, but the truth is that I am finishing this article four months after the sleepless night in question, and the letter asking me to write it, from George Miller of the University of Delaware, arrived almost two years ago, so for all I know Mr. Miller has managed to assemble his textbook on revision without me.

Oh, well. That's how it goes when you start thinking about revision. That's the danger of it, in fact. You can spend so much time thinking about how to switch things around that the main event has passed you by. But it doesn't matter. Because by the time you reach middle age, you want more than anything for things not to come to an end; and as long as you're still revising, they don't.

I'm sorry to end so morbidly—dancing as I am around the subject of death—but there are advantages to it. For one thing, I have managed to move fairly effortlessly and logically from the beginning of this piece through the middle and to the end. And for another, I am able to close with an exhortation, something I rarely manage, which is this: Revise now, before it's too late.

November, 1986